BUILD
UNIVERSES

Vincent A. Amos
(a.k.a. D'Vinny)

Wisdom From Above The Clouds – 66 Daily Meditations

© 2021 **Europe Books** | London
www.europebooks.co.uk – info@europebooks.co.uk

ISBN 979-12-201-1032-7
First edition: July 2021

Distribution for the United Kingdom: **Vine House Distribution ltd**

Printed for Italy by Rotomail Italia
Finito di stampare nel mese di luglio 2021
presso Rotomail Italia S.p.A. - Vignate (MI)

Wisdom From Above The Clouds –
66 Daily Meditations

Author's Note

This portion of the book "Wisdom From Above The Clouds" contains "66 Daily Meditations" dealing with common place issues on today's landscape of events. Each event or topic is set to Biblical scripture. All sixty-six books in the Holy Bible are utilized because each book of the Bible, regardless of its length is of equal importance.

May this religious literary work bring a certain amount of delightful joy, warm comfort, and restful peace to each reader. Each topic can be expanded to a 200-page book with minimal effort. Notwithstanding this fact, the length of correspondence on each topic was kept to an enjoyable; but yet informative length which gets directly to the point without wasting the reader's valuable time. This book can be used as a supplement to normal Bible reading. It is designed to increase one's understanding on the various issues in life from a biblical perspective.

Enjoy this work; for I have given it my heart. I shall look forward upon seeing each reader when we rejoin with The Father in heaven and enjoy paradise to no end. Stay blessed by God.

From my heart to yours,

D'Vinny

Day 1 | Marriage

"... made He a woman and brought her unto the man."
Genesis 2:22

Marriage is holy matrimony which belongs to God.
D'Vinny

The Creator spoke everything into existence; however, when it came to humanity God physically produced both man and woman by the labor of His own hands, creating them in His own image. Therefore, man and woman are God's direct representatives on earth.

The act of marriage is the method established by God as the means of procreation for humanity. In the beginning, Adam and Eve were joined together in the first wedding ceremony. Given that God created marriage, it is sacred, honorable, and accountable to Him.

A marriage has to be committed to God before the individuals in the marriage can be successfully committed to each other. It is important to remember that marriage is an act of spiritual devotion. Only a sincere understanding of that fact will allow the union to become an expression of divine glory which shall always and forever be an inseparable bond, keeping the couple together.

A marriage will last as long as both husband and wife hold onto God first, before they attempt to hold onto each other. The rationale is straightforward: in a godly marriage with godly people, it is He who brings both male and female together, same as He did with

Adam and Eve. Therefore, only a proper relationship with Him will keep the couple together in marriage.

Many problems can surface during a marriage. Adam and Eve went through multiple disasters simultaneously. They were rich, with all their needs met; then they quickly became poor. They had a home; then they were evicted and became homeless. They were blessed with eternal life; then they became punished with the curse of death. They were happy; later they experienced the sadness of paradise lost. They were in the state of perfect fellowship with God; then they became creatures of sin.

There were differences. There was blame. Yet, they stayed married.

The meditative point upon which we must reflect is that everyone has a reason as to why divorce is the best recourse. However, withstanding the temptation, we see that God is the only One who can make a difference in a marriage, especially when both parties seek a blessing of marriage redemption from God. Long-lasting, mutual respect in a marriage can only be achieved—and persistently maintained—when both parties have a love for God and invite Him to be a part of their marriage. It was God who created man and woman; therefore, only He truly knows about both genders.

May all marriages find and enjoy the blessings of God. Stay Blessed.

D'Vinny

Day 2 | Love

". . . God is love; and he that dwelleth in love dwelleth in God, and God in him."

John 4:16

The myth of the world: love and sex are the same thing.
D'Vinny

God shall be always and forever the Creator, and the objective of man is to emulate the One who created him. The characteristic of love reflects the very essence of God.

Man was made lower than the angels in heaven. Nonetheless, man is God's only creature on earth with a soul—the very breath of God. It is the divine part of us. Consequently, man must attempt to reflect his Creator. Understanding the fact that God is love is the first step toward the process of "Creator emulation."

God's love for us is without conditions. He is committed to mankind—not merely as earthly clay vessels of ashes and dust. More importantly, God loves the total man—the body, soul, and spirit. Therefore, God concerns Himself with the physical needs of man's natural existence as well as man's spiritual needs for holistic existence.

God's love is free; it bears no financial cost. It is reflective of the character of God. Throughout the timeline of man's habitation on earth, God repeatedly displayed His love for an often-disobedient mankind. The flood of Noah was a display of God's love, in that the entire human race was not eradicated from the planet. The greatest display of love is found in the scripture: "For God so loved the world, that he gave his only-begotten Son, that whosoever believeth in him should not perish, but have everlasting life" (John 3:16).

This scripture is known as the "little bible within the Bible." God loved man enough to provide for full atonement of man's sins through His Son, Jesus. In the same chapter the Bible clearly tells us the purpose of Jesus' earthly mission: "For God sent not his Son into the world to condemn the world; but that the world through Him might be saved" (John 3:17).

The concept of salvation for the individual's soul is based on a person's personal acceptance of Jesus. There is self-condemnation for the person who does not believe. In the same chapter we also find: "He that believeth in him is not condemned: but he that believeth not is condemned already, because he hath not believed in the name of the only begotten Son of God" (John 3:18).

Let us come to know God through His Son, Jesus, and we will have more love than we can bear. Our understanding of true love will be made complete.

Experience God's love so that your soul will be full. Stay blessed.

D'Vinny

Day 3 | Salvation

"That if thou shalt confess with thy mouth the Lord Jesus, and shalt believe in thine heart that God hath raised him from the dead, thou shalt be saved. For with the heart man believeth unto righteousness; and with the mouth confession is made unto salvation."

Romans 10:9-10

Nothing is more important than where the soul will spend eternity.

D'Vinny

Salvation is a spiritual concept which focuses on heaven as the final resting place for the soul. Salvation is attained during the time of earthly existence. This physical state is the condition in which the soul, the spirit, and the body are jointly residing within a living organism.

Once death occurs, there is a separation of these three elements. The soul and the spirit must leave the body and the body will go back to the earth from whence it was taken. This is the reason why, during a funeral service, the minister will say, "Earth to earth, ashes to ashes, and dust to dust." The spirit always goes back to the Father who gave it. And the soul will either go to heaven or to hell.

Heaven is the loving place of fellowship with God; whereas hell is the abode of Satan—a place of eternal doom, punishment, and damnation. A saved soul should be the objective of anyone who loves, honors, and fears God. The desire is to forever remain in the blessed presence of God for all eternity.

Salvation is something that is not attainable by tangible means; in other words, salvation is not a physical product. Salvation cannot be bought with money, gold, stocks, or bonds. It is a spiritual gift which Christians believe as taught by the Scriptures: "Jesus saith unto him, I am the way, the truth, and the life: no man cometh unto the Father, but by me" (John 14:6), additionally, "And brought them out, and said, Sirs, what must I do to be saved? And they said, Believe on the Lord Jesus Christ, and thou shalt be saved, and thy house" (Acts 16:30-31).

Salvation is a gift of God which is offered freely to all through the redemptive work of God the Son—Jesus Christ. Jesus paid for it all. He alone permitted salvation by following the will of the Father, by dying on a cross for the sins of humanity. Through Jesus, the penalty of sin—total separation from God—has been eliminated. Jesus was obedient and His act of atonement, which literally means "at one with," served as a conduit for the salvation of humanity.

It took Christ's precious blood to be shed, and the power of His glorious resurrection, to allow man's soul the opportunity for spiritual peace and entry into heaven.

Man has obtained nothing until he has obtained salvation from God. Stay blessed.

D'Vinny

Day 4 | Table Grace

"And when He had taken the five loaves and the two fishes, He looked up to heaven and blessed."

Mark 6:41

We must continuously give respectful thanks to God.
D'Vinny

All too often the people of industrialized nations of the world have a tendency to take the consumption of goods for granted. The grocery stores, farmer's markets, fruit stands, commissaries, and 24-hour mega-warehouse-type stores are filled with food brought in from all over the world.

One hundred years ago, even the very rich could only get the fruit which was in season. Today, because of advanced technology, globalization, and international trade, the world has a significant advantage. The agricultural growing seasons are no longer a constraint. Apples, peaches, bananas, oranges, etc., are always in season somewhere. Food items can be harvested and quickly transported by a combination of sophisticated shipment methods—thus, being delivered fresh for consumption.

There is one act which can demonstrate our reverence, humbleness, and obedience. This is the special prayer said unto God before a meal is consumed, known as table grace. Humanity must never forget: "Pray without ceasing" (1 Thessalonians 5:17).

Table grace is a specific prayer that reminds us that food is needed in order to live, and, moreover, that all food comes from God. The Lord gives the sunshine and the rain. He allows the soil and the climate to produce all types of fruits, vegetables, and grain needed for all of his creatures. "So then neither is he that planteth anything, neither he that watereth; but God that giveth the increase" (1 Corinthians 3:7).

At each meal, table grace reminds us that we are dependent upon God. It reinforces the fact that we are limited in nature. Each meal or feast could be our last. Not even the next day, or next hour, of our life is guaranteed. Therefore, table grace expresses thankfulness for the present food at the present point in time.

Jesus gave a beautiful example of looking to heaven and giving thanks unto God for the food that the five thousand male heads-of-household, and each of their wives and children, were going to receive. All religious people, whether at home, on a picnic, or in a restaurant, should follow Jesus' example and give thanks for the food they are about to receive.

Table grace allows the supremacy of God to be acknowledged in the life of the believer.

Enjoy every meal with the blessing of God. Stay Blessed.

D'Vinny

Day 5 | Disappointment

"Therefore, my beloved brethren, be ye stedfast, unmoveable, always abounding in the work of the Lord, forasmuch as ye know that your labour is not in vain in the Lord."

1 Corinthians 15:58

Let all disappointments be brief and temporary.

D'Vinny

Very often there are situations beyond our control. Sometimes, even with the most meticulous attention to detail we cannot avoid the vicissitudes of life. An undesirable outcome can lead to low self-esteem and low self-worth. The "why me?" question is continuously self-posited.

If this is left unchecked, the person will develop a defeatist mentality which can lead to depression and, in some cases, suicide. Disappointment occurs at unexpected times, and primarily its appearance and duration are without warning. Each person has to understand that disappointment is temporary.

Jesus knew and understood disappointment. Judas Iscariot betrayed Jesus with a kiss. Peter denied Jesus three times. Thomas doubted the very presence of Jesus, even when He appeared to him face to face. The people of Israel displayed little faith on multiple occasions. His very people rejected him. The citizens in other regions of Israel had severe reservations about him. The saying was quite common and often repeated: "Can anything good come out of Nazareth?"

Nevertheless, Jesus overcame this situation and all other negative encounters by staying spiritual. Likewise, people of today can emulate Jesus and avoid the possibility of being disappointed by staying spiritual and remaining in a constant state of prayer.

We must follow Jesus' example if we are to triumph over disappointment. Disappointment must be met with prayer and faith in God. Yes, it is fully perceived that problems in life will occur; but, the Christian person knows that God is able to resolve any situation.

God does not have to do anything for anybody by 1300 hours or 1:00 o'clock p.m. on next Tuesday afternoon. Whenever God shows up it is the right time. God will never fail and He is too wise to make a mistake. He always shows up at the right time, at the right place, and with the right blessing for the right person.

What we often fail to recognize is that the waiting period is a blessing. This is a hollowed time; it is a time of spiritual reflection while the individual is waiting on God to work a miracle.

God will give you a blessing which will dilute the effects of disappointment. Stay blessed.

D'Vinny

Day 6 | Friendship

". . . And Ahaziah the son of Jehoram king of Judah went down to see Joram the son of Ahab in Jezreel, because he was sick."

2 Kings 8:29b

Let us be friendly at all times.

D'Vinny

All people require some level of human contact in order to maintain a healthy social equilibrium. This is true whether the person is an outgoing, lively extrovert, or an isolationist who is introverted in nature. Human existence becomes more enjoyable when two or more people forge the special bond of friendship.

Friends help to add more value and meaning to life. They make the great times and celebrations such as weddings, birthdays, retirements, and other key events better. They also help navigate through the storms—from a dead car battery or a flat tire, to the death of a spouse or long-term hospital stay. During adverse times friendship is vital.

Everyone whom we know is not our friend. It is imperative to realize that there is a difference between a friend and an acquaintance. In truth, most people only have two or three perfect solid trustworthy close friends.

A close friend that is true is one to whom we can tell all our troubles. A friend will never broadcast information told to them in confidence. A true friend will never let anyone know that he knew the information even when it became public knowledge; in other words, he would act like he is hearing the information for the very first time, regardless of the outcome.

Friendship starts with the person we see in the mirror. The Bible teaches that in order to have a friend we must show ourselves to *be* a friend. Therefore, friendship has the origin of self-examination, self-accountability, and self-assessment.

If there is an issue with understanding the nature of friendship, then we must receive the scriptures and realize that ". . . there is a friend that sticketh closer than a brother" (Proverbs 18:24). Enjoy the words as expressed by the Gospel Hymnist, Fanny Crosby: *Blessed Assurance*. And say with faithful gratitude that *Jesus Is Mine*.

Enjoy the continuous blessings of Jesus' friendship. Stay blessed.

D'Vinny

Day 7 | Crime

"By swearing, and lying, and killing, and stealing, and committing adultery, they break out, and blood toucheth blood."

Hosea 4:2

All crime starts with temptation.

D'Vinny

Ultimately, all crime that occurs in society is the manifestation of sin. Crime is caused by the convergence of three things.

1. The desire to commit the act.
2. The opportunity or target which is available.
3. A criminal means or methodology, i.e., a way to carry out the crime.

Typically, when those three factors intersect, along with the absence of Godly Christian principles, some type of crime will happen. Sin, when perpetrated against another person, against property, or against society in general, has a selfish or self-centered modus operandi associated with it—the "I" factor.

The Lord God set the standard for human behavior many times throughout the Bible. In the fourth chapter of Genesis, God forewarned Cain that sin was about to overtake him and control his physical body. Cain should have felt love, care, and concern for his brother Abel. Nonetheless, whatever positive feelings that existed were quickly overtaken by his unwarranted rage. This was due to his undisciplined nature and violent temper.

Thereafter, the first murder in human history was recorded.

God, Himself was the sole author of the Ten Commandments. He wrote them in stone so that they would not be changed. These codified statutes set guidelines for human behavior; they set limits on the foolish concept of total, unrestrained freedom. These laws were not written for the achievement of salvation. They were written so that they would be followed in order to please God and keep society in order. The Ten Commandments are a restriction of total free will which has the positive result to allow man to make the right personal choices in life for the benefit of his individual relationship with God as well as his fellow man.

Very sadly, crime does exist in our society. However, there is hope that God will help to see us through any given situation. Also for those persons who have been innocent victims of crime, the Christian principle of forgiveness is the fastest way to a speedy recovery of spiritual healing.

God has the answers to and the blessings for any situation. Stay blessed.

D'Vinny

Day 8 | Benediction

"The LORD bless thee, and keep thee: The LORD make his face shine upon thee, and be gracious unto thee: The LORD lift up his countenance upon thee, and give thee peace."

Numbers 6:24-26

The Benediction is the least understood part of the church service.

D'Vinny

The benediction is usually a short prayer said by a minister or religious authority on behalf of a Christian congregation. It is an important part of the service because it is the final event on the agenda. This is the last appeal to God for the people gathered together.

Benediction is a request to God for His blessings of love, mercy, grace, safety, and companionship of the Holy Spirit. It is done at the end of the service, before the believers depart and go their separate ways to serve God in the normal endeavors of their daily lives. Many churches will have the inscription "Enter to worship, depart to serve" written on their church bulletins for this reason.

The benediction is the last religious act of worship which will keep the church family and the extended religious assembly under the unmerited favor of God until they meet again the following week. No one should have a negative or nonchalant attitude toward the benediction, to willfully leave church early prior to the benediction being given. It is an important blessing which everyone needs, individually and as a whole congregation.

Everyone needs a blessing of safety. Given that most people drive to and from church, the drunk driver needs to be kept by the Hand of the Holy Spirit on his side of the road.

The benediction reminds us that we need to carry God with us and live like we belong to God, especially outside the church. It is all too common that some people are only religious inside the church, and outside completely void of any righteous knowledge or understanding of God. This is a continuous challenge which requires self-examination, the subsequent improvement of which should be evident in the person's overt persona.

May all benedictions be spiritual, reverent, and joyfully appreciated in order to attain a greater closeness with God.

Enjoy the blessing of every benediction which you receive. Stay blessed.

D'Vinny

Day 9 | Lying

"For many deceivers are entered into the world, who confess not that Jesus Christ is come in the flesh. This is a deceiver and an antichrist."

2 John 1:7

All lies will become exposed.

D'Vinny

Everything in society centers on accuracy of information. The old axiom is still applicable today: "A person's word is their bond." Our spoken word binds us to a given situation. If deliberate misrepresentation of a fact occurs by way of a person's deceptive speech, the results could be catastrophic. Given a scenario in which the pilot of a 747 jumbo jet were to ask the head aircraft mechanic about a recent maintenance inspection, and the mechanic were to relay a false report, the lives of many passengers, as well as people on the ground, would be in jeopardy.

Lying is a common sin which most people learn as children. Once a person learns to lie and learns to utilize lying as a method to avoid a difficult situation, then it will become a part of the person's character. The person will be labeled by the sin and called a liar. We are what we do? We become known by the things which we do, and the acts which we commit. If we often lie, then we become inseparable from the act; thus, we are labeled.

Sadly, some adults have not yet learned the value of telling the truth and having an honest reputation. They still have the same character as the young lying child, because that sin was never corrected by the three great agents of influence: home, church, and school.

Reputations have been ruined, feelings have been hurt, marriages have been destroyed, lives have been lost—all due to a person's improper use of the tongue. Telling the truth was especially important in the past. In Biblical times a person could be put to death on the testimony of two eyewitnesses (see Deuteronomy 17).

God's commandment which prohibits lying states: "Thou shalt not bear false witness against thy neighbor" (Exodus 20:16). God also repeatedly forbids untruthful speech in the Book of Proverbs.

The person who has a problem with telling the truth must come to understand the spiritual consequences of lying. A person cannot lie their way into God's heaven; but they can lie their way into the devil's hell.

The truth is a blessing; enjoy it when both good and bad information are given. Stay blessed.

D'Vinny

Day 10 | Money

"For the love of money is the root of all evil: which while some coveted after, they have erred from the faith, and pierced themselves through with many sorrows."

1 Timothy 6:10

Too many things are overemphasized in society; money is certainly one of them.

D'Vinny

The use of money as a financial instrument has been a complicated issue ever since the nations of the world disbanded the barter system. Money serves multiple roles in an economy. It is a means of exchange, a store of value, and a unit of account. Each of these is important in order for a country to have a stable business climate.

One of the most interesting things said about money is the famous quote from the motion picture *Wall Street*, wherein, the father gave his son the advice, "Money is not something that you need, if you are not going to be here tomorrow." This quote is from a fictional movie which was meant to entertain, but we see a parallel in Jesus' teachings as recorded in Matthew 16: "For what is a man profited, if he shall gain the whole world, and lose his own soul? Or what shall a man give in exchange for his soul?"

The soul is the God-given part of a mortal man. Unlike money—which has limited temporal value—the soul has eternal value. A soul which has received and accepted salvation from God through His Son, Jesus, goes to heaven. An unsaved soul goes to hell and is forever cast away from the presence of God.

27

It is realized that physical needs are important. Abraham Maslow clearly articulated this fact with his "Hierarchy of Needs" model. The physical needs are primordial: food, clothing, and shelter. These needs are basic and must be met in order to survive; nevertheless, an absence of these needs, or the lack of money to procure them, does not justify sinful, corrupt, or immoral means to obtain them.

Understandingly, in this present-day global economy, there is a necessity to have funding to meet certain daily requirements. Using the principle of brevity, the table below provides a clear enlightenment of the original entity, as depicted on the left side, and the desired objective for money as pay off or economic return, as depicted on the right side of the table. Each entity must earn a sufficient pre-determined objective in order to achieve its goals of sustainment and survival.

MONETARY NEEDS MODEL	
ENTITY	MONETARY OBJECTIVE
Workers	Wages
Land	Rent
Money	Interest
Business	Profit
Government	Taxes
Church	Tithes
University	Alumni Contributions
Charities	Donations
Capital	Rate of Return
Farmers	Harvest
Bonds	Yield
National Economy	Productivity

Table 1. Monetary Needs Model

Everyone must follow God through the teachings of His Son, Jesus. Money must be placed in its proper perspective. The old adage is true, all money is not good money. It is the condition of the soul, not the condition of the stock portfolio or bank account, which receives the interest of God. When life is over, no one can buy his way into heaven.

Enjoy the blessings of God, and money will follow. Stay blessed.

D'Vinny

Day 11 | Wisdom

"And account that the longsuffering of our Lord is salvation; even as our beloved brother Paul also according to the wisdom given unto him hath written unto you . . ."

2 Peter 3:15

True wisdom uses decision making which pleases God.
D'Vinny

The Book of Proverbs is viewed as the book of wisdom in the Bible. However, the entire Bible deals with wisdom, both wise and unwise decisions made, and the consequences thereof are experienced.

There are two types: the wisdom of God and the wisdom of man. The latter is often emotional, short-sighted, and limited in scope, whereas Divine wisdom—the wisdom of God—is incomprehensibly higher. The ultimate application of that wisdom is during the making of decisions. Hopefully, in most cases, decisions are made upon wisdom which has a foundation in some rational basis. Whether we succeed or continue to struggle is determined upon the decisions which we make.

A good example is in the realm of financial decision making. It is wise to start saving for retirement at the onset of a career, as opposed to waiting until two years before retirement. The Divine truth is that most people do not need more money; they first need to make wise, Godly decisions with the money they already have. Thereafter, God will bless them with more money in the future.

The Bible says, if any person lacks wisdom, ". . . let him ask God, who will give wisdom liberally and upbraideth not" (James 1:5). When decisions are taken to God in prayer, His wisdom often meets or exceeds the circumstances at hand.

Often times, these four terms are used interchangeably: *educated, smart, intelligent,* and *wise.* This is misuse, as these are distinctly different concepts.

Educated means that someone possesses proof of attending an academic institution and completing the requirements of the curriculum, usually obtaining a degree.

Smart means that a person is able to grasp information quickly, retaining it for current and future use. Smartness, if left unchecked, can be dangerous. It can lead a person to a false sense of superiority and an arrogant disposition. Consider the ten-year-old student who thinks he is smarter than both his teacher and his parents. Consider the taxpayer who thinks he can outsmart the IRS and federal tax laws. Both of these individuals will likely encounter a painful and regretful day of reckoning.

Intelligent means that someone has an admirable cerebral capacity, demonstrably superior when compared to their peers. Both the mental faculty and the aptitude potential of the individual are extraordinary. Although intelligence and smartness are similar, there is a slight difference when it comes to the application of decision making. The student who drops out of high school may be intelligent, but his decision is not smart.

Wisdom, especially Divine wisdom, is given from God in heaven to the requestor. This person does not rely on his own understanding, but seeks direction and leadership as guided by the Hand of God. Wisdom brings all three of the other qualities together and gently places them under His guidance. It is the wisdom of

God which keeps the individual in position for success, by keeping him away from the sins of laziness, arrogance, pride, and selfishness. Divine wisdom will help one avoid the negative traps of life.

A brilliant surgeon who is educated, smart, and intelligent, but who cannot get out of bed because he is lazy and always misses appointments will have a limited career. God's wisdom is necessary for us to be wholesome individuals—fully balanced to encounter and excel with the challenges of life.

The world must learn to let the wisdom of God reign supreme in all things, leading us to a world of peace and His continued blessings.

Enjoy the divine wisdom which only comes from God. Stay blessed.

D'Vinny

Day 12 | Joy

". . . neither be ye sorry; for the joy of the Lord is your strength."

Nehemiah 8:10

Only God can give the world great joy.

D'Vinny

Often times the word joy is used in conjunction with things which are sinful. There is a twenty-four-hour city in the southwestern desert which has the nickname "Sin City." The saying which encourages a climate of sin is: "What happens in Vegas, stays in Vegas."

Although this saying is used as a marketing tool to encourage tourism from all over the globe, it also brings a false sense of the word "joy." This limited viewpoint implies that happiness is abundant as long as other people are having fun and filled with excitement, and that their euphoria is instantaneously transferable.

This is not the case. Earthly joy carries the appearance of happiness and satisfaction, but—as we often find out—this type of joy is cheap, shallow, and has to be constantly replenished.

Christians have a greater comprehension of joy. True joy is not dependent on anything of man. It gently rests upon God's grace and mercy. The lyrics of the gospel song are still true: "This joy which I have / the world did not give it to me / and the world cannot take it away."

Spiritual joy is internal; it is a blessed state wherein the person allows God to touch his heart, mind, and spirit. It focuses on God's Son, Jesus, who is our High Priest, who sits at the right Hand of the Father. This type of joy can only be bought with faith in God.

The world knows joy as entertainment, excitement, merriment, and socialization. Thus, the world pursues joy in the form of shopping malls, club memberships, cinemas, plastic surgery, etc. These things are fine—they have a specific place in society's culture. But earthly joy is always situational in its dependency. The variables which constitute this dependency are on the physical side of this universe.

A Christian's joy is centered upon God and the result is one of tranquility and peace. Let everyone come closer to God to receive His incomparable joy—one which lasts forever.

Only God can give true joy. Stay blessed.

D'Vinny

Day 13 | Patience

"Better is the end of a thing than the beginning thereof; and the patient in spirit is better than the proud in spirit."

Ecclesiastes 7:8

Patience is the world's most effective free medicine.

D'Vinny

Many people associate certain qualities with success: talent, loyalty, intelligence, optimism, steadfastness, etc. However, there is one key Christian attribute which is lacking today. Moreover, this attribute has been lacking in its successful application throughout history.

Patience is placing our desire to control time into the Hands of God. We have a tendency to want things to happen exactly when we feel they should, in order to meet our perceived ideas of a given circumstance. A Christian understands that time belongs to God and that when we try to rush it a disaster is often the result.

One of the most effective parenting skills is to teach our children the importance of patience. Children, on their own, will try to grow up too quickly and they will attempt to do things before their time. There is a reason why society does not allow a thirteen-year-old to operate a motor vehicle. The maturity level simply is not there. A car's accelerator can quickly become the accelerator of death. Consequently, many lives would be lost on the roads and highways.

There once was a young man whom God called to preach the Gospel at the age of sixteen. He started off as a good preacher; nevertheless, his zeal for success led him to desire the hastening of his abilities. Therefore, he prayed to God to allow him to preach with the power, control, and conviction of one who had been preaching for twenty years. God granted his request. Thus, when the audience next heard the young thirty-six-year-old preacher, they were amazed that the young man sounded just like he had been preaching for twenty years.

It is important to know that mankind cannot rush the Hand of God. Typically, when people rush life to achieve a predetermined goal, they have a tendency to ruin things in the process. The force of evil uses impatience as a pathway toward sin. God will urge you to wait six months until there is enough money saved to buy the watch and pay for it with cash. The force of evil says shoplifting makes it available right now. God will urge you to work and save for the new car. The force of evil says a 9 mm and a quick carjack will work immediately.

A lack of patience, when fully manifested, will lead to sin and its unfortunate consequences. The use of patience represents one of the many characteristics of God. Our personal character is improved through patience.

Waiting on God gives us the blessing. Stay blessed.
D'Vinny

Day 14 | Parenting

"And the name of the man was Elimelech, and the name of his wife Naomi, and the name of his two sons Mahlon and Chilion, Ephrathites of Bethlehemjudah . . ."

Ruth 1:2

Being a parent is the greatest honor that God can give two people.

D'Vinny

Children are a gift and a blessing from God. Children represent new life and a continuation of a family. If no children are born, then the family name slowly fades from the annals of time. Thereafter, with the erosion of the family, neighborhood, community, state, and nation will die out over time and eventually cease to exist.

Biologically, male and females may engage in copulation; however, the physical transaction is fruitless unless God blesses the reproductive system within the institution of marriage. It is important to keep in mind that man can do nothing without God.

God has entrusted the parents, along with the secondary assistance of the grandparents, to rear their children in a religious, moral, and socially upstanding manner. Children have to be taught the difference between right and wrong and each child is a mirror of the household's values. A well-trained and well-behaved child is a positive reflection upon Godly parents. Conversely, an undisciplined child who is rude and without self-control is a reflection of the absence of positive attributes in his family. If the family follows the creed of "do whatever you want" then the child's behavior will reflect that.

God holds the parents directly accountable for the rearing of children. Parents are the primary arbitrators of a child's conduct, both at home and in the public realm. It is easier to shape and mold a child who is four years old than it is when he or she is fourteen. One of the contributing factors to the increase in prison populations is that morals and values which should have been taught early on by the parents are being taught at the age of eighteen in the state superior court—by the judge delivering a sentence.

It is easier to guide a child than it is to repair an adult. Allegorically, it is easier to mold wet cement which has not yet solidified than to mold old, hard, sun-dried cement which has long taken solid form. Most people would agree that the latter is a nearly impossible task.

The majority of modern societies have a democratic form of government. The word "democratic" literally means "rule of the people," and any society that wishes to increase its economic standard of living and overall quality of life has to develop its future generation of citizens. It is the aggregate quality of the citizenry that will determine the future course of the nation. In this same way, if we are to increase the standard of God-centered living in our families, then the child-rearing skills of each set of parents, as led by the Hand of God, will ensure this direction.

Blessed be the children, and the parents who follow God's Word to rear them. Stay blessed.

D'Vinny

Day 15 | Death

A Psalm of Praise at the Time of Death

1. Who can understand the mysterious and wondrous works of God?
2. The Lord, in His infinite wisdom always makes the right decisions.
3. God knows each of us, and those who live according to His purpose shall be called home to rejoice with God at the time of death.
4. Death is a portal for the righteous, a conduit to eternal life.
5. This world is not our home, for we have a building not made by hand. We have a home of perfection made by the wisdom of God.
6. Rejoice at the great homegoing! Let there be a celebration of new life and of a saved soul who is at peace with the Father.
7. The wicked who did not know God did not have this assurance. Their fate is eternal damnation separated from God.
8. Those who know God, who have died with their sins forgiven, are blessed among blessed.
9. Thank God for His Son Jesus, who made salvation possible.
10. Praise be to God at all times, in life, and death, for the great things which He has done. Praise be to God. Let the whole earth praise God!

Death takes on a different meaning when it touches a family member or a close friend of the concerned; beyond grief, let us give thanks to God for the blessing of each person's life. Stay blessed.

D'Vinny

Day 16 | Thy Neighbor

*"For all the law is fulfilled in one word, even in this;
Thou shalt love thy neighbor as thyself."*

Galatians 5:14

*Let the love for thy neighbor help to send you to heaven,
as opposed to the alternative.*

D'Vinny

There is a natural tendency to show kindness toward someone who is of the same race, religion, and social or economic class as ourselves. People tend to like people who are like themselves. Other people, those of a different culture or social stratum, tend to receive treatment which is different.

God expects us to see the humanity in each of our fellow men, and to treat them like they are the handiwork of the Creator. The scriptures contain the highest form of codified law, which demand that we treat our neighbor as we treat ourselves. This straightforward mandate has often been overlooked throughout the course of human history. Many of the world's social ills—poverty, starvation, crime, political conflict, *et al*—in part originate from the violation of the Biblical principle of loving one's neighbor as thyself.

The law as represented by the Ten Commandments consists of two parts. The first part deals with man's relationship with God. This is eloquently expressed in the first four commandments:

Thou shalt have no other gods before Me.
Thou shalt not make a graven image.
Thou shalt not use the Lord's name in vain.

41

Remember the Sabbath Day and keep it holy.

These verses of scripture designate how man, in his sinful state, is to relate to a holy God. These scriptures direct man's behavior and actions toward his God.

The second part of the law deals with man's relationship to man. God has told us how we are to relate to each other:

Honor thy father and thy mother.
Thou shalt not kill.
Thou shalt not commit adultery.
Thou shalt not steal.
Thou shalt not bear false witness against thy neighbor.
Thou shalt not covet anything of thy neighbor.

If the various societies of the world would understand and govern their behavior according to God's Word, this world would be a much different and much better place.

Treat all neighbors like they are a blessing from God. Stay blessed.

D'Vinny

Day 17 | Anxiety

"The waters compassed me about, even to the soul: the depth closed me round about, the weeds were wrapped about my head."

Jonah 2:5

Replace the act of worrying with faith and God will do the rest.

D'Vinny

The modern world is full of time saving conveniences. Automatic garage door openers, microwave ovens, cellular telephones, laptop computers, satellite communications, laparoscopic surgery, remote controls, etc., have contributed to an unthinkably high quality of life for many people.

Our society, with all its electronic gadgetry, has been conditioned to demand everything instantly. It used to take ninety days to cross the Atlantic Ocean by boat. Now it takes five days to get from New York City to London by way of an ocean liner, and just eight hours by jet aircraft. Six weeks is too long to wait for an income tax return; with electronic funds transfer, the tax refund can be deposited in five days.

When things don't happen as quickly as we would like, anxiety begins, and we start to worry. Most of the things that we worry about are not even problems. In truth, the act of worrying is the real problem. It is wasted energy. It solves nothing and is wholly unproductive, usually resulting in a deep malaise. Simply put, a state of anxiety is not valuable. It is value*less*.

Pray. Do not worry.

We must remember this. Prayer is a Christian's best weapon against the enemy. Anxiety comes from the forces of evil; it exists to confuse, bewilder, and dismay. If left unchecked, it can erode a person's faith, because the person will begin to doubt the power of God. The act of prayer is the answer, to turn the condition over to Him. Prayer changes things; it nourishes the soul through Divine communication. If the Christian person prays, then there is no need to worry, because God has the situation in His Hands. Nothing on earth or in heaven is too hard for God (see Genesis 18).

If one does not pray, then there is cause for worry. But the temporary situation at hand is not the major concern. The real concern should be why the person is not in fellowship with God about the future resting place of one's soul.

Remain in a state of blessedness and God will handle all worries. Stay blessed.

D'Vinny

Day 18 | Greed

"Woe unto them! for they have gone in the way of Cain, and ran greedily after the error of Balaam for reward, and perished in the gainsaying of Core."

Jude 1:11

The demonic force of greed has often suppressed the better judgment of man.

D'Vinny

Greed has long been recognized as one of "The Seven Deadly Sins." This is a secular term derived from the sixth chapter of the Book of Proverbs and applied to a group of sins which are very common and easy to commit.

Greed is a cancerous condition of the spirit in which a person is never fully satisfied with the tangible, material things that God has allowed him to possess. Having a good car that is in excellent mechanical condition is not enough. The person has the burning desire to get the newest, latest-and-greatest automotive machine in order to attain a superficial sense of elevation above others. The 4,000-square-foot house, even though the children are grown, and the grandchildren come to visit twice a year, is not enough. The 9,000-square-foot house best reflects the individual's status and level of social and economic achievement.

Greed also extends to the intangible as well. There is a false need driven by sin to sing better, walk better, talk better, look better, and absorb all of the attention one can summon.

The real problem is that greed is a demon which can never be satisfied. One good wife who the Holy Spirit has provided is not enough for some men. A modern creed of many: "Thou shalt not get caught."

Greed if it is left unchecked, will override morals, destroy self-discipline, and take deep root inside a person's soul. It will deter the infected person from heaven and lead him down the road to the abyss of hell.

The solution to greed is that of advanced prevention. A Christian must be armed with the Word of God, allowing the person to stay within God's blessed righteousness. Greed can be conquered by maintaining a pious focus on the One who is able to overcome all sin, evil, and the temptations of life.

The blessings of God will nullify the temptation of greed. Stay blessed.

D'Vinny

Day 19 | Stripping

"Whoso loveth wisdom rejoiceth his father: but he that keepeth company with harlots spendeth his substance."
Proverbs 29:3

The Lord views stripping as prostitution.
D'Vinny

The objective is money. The tools are simple: loud music, flashing lights, and perfectly oiled, well-shaped bodies of either gender moving rhythmically, while simultaneously removing all of their clothing, one piece at a time.

In this environment, two types of stripping take place. The first is when the person removes their clothes. The second is when the audience gets stripped of its money. It is still true that "a fool and his gold are soon parted."

Nudity before the "fall of man" was not sinful. Nakedness was a blessed state of contentment. Adam and Eve, the first man and the first woman, were naked and not ashamed (see Genesis 2). Subsequently, after the first sin occurred, Adam and Eve discovered that they were naked and hid themselves from the presence of God. It is at this point that a public display of overt nakedness became shameful, because sin had entered the world.

Nudity, whether it exists in adult films, magazines, movies, or other forms of media, is displeasing to God. All who are involved, provider or lustful consumer, are engaging in a type of behavior that puts heaven out of reach—and brings hell closer. It is true that money can be made in this type of activity; however, all money is not good money. We are instructed to "be ... not greedy of filthy lucre . . ." (see 1 Timothy 3). This means that whether stripping is legal or not, it is still immoral, sinful, and representative of many of the vile pagan practices of ancient times.

No short-term financial gain is worth the spiritual costs. Stripping leads to the loss of self-worth, self-dignity, self-esteem, and future self-actualization. It gives nothing worthwhile, but rather takes away the very essence of each participant. The name of stripping explains the condition as well as the effect; stripping is a stripped job.

Remain close to God without the burden of sin. Stay blessed.

D'Vinny

Day 20 | Angels

"And to you who are troubled rest with us, when the Lord Jesus shall be revealed from heaven with his mighty angels."

2 Thessalonians 1:7

The work and the mission of angels represent the divine glory of God.

D'Vinny

Angels are heavenly beings created by the divine Hand of God. They have several important duties in their service to Him. Supernatural beings who are not bound by the physical limitations of the natural world, angels do not age, get sick, take vacations, and they do not retire. They are not constrained by time or space.

Angels are divine messengers from God. They have appeared directly in the presence of humans to deliver a word directly from heaven. It was the angel Gabriel who told both Mary and Joseph of their future concerning the Messiah. Angels are ministerial spirits. A clear depiction of this is when Jesus had finished fasting for forty days and nights; immediately thereafter, He fought off the temptations of Satan. Once Satan failed and departed from Jesus, angels came to Jesus and ministered unto Him.

Angels are protectors and guardians. Sadly, once Adam and Eve had sinned in the Garden of Eden, God evicted them from this estate of paradise. Guardian angels known as cherubim were placed at the entrance of the Garden with a flaming sword to prevent anyone from entering (see Genesis 3:24).

Angels are spiritually able to fight against Satan. Michael the Archangel won the dispute with the devil, as Satan tried to take physical possession of the body of Moses, by saying, "The Lord rebuke thee" (Jude 1:9).

In our modern society, it is important to understand that angels are still present among us. We should always be careful how we treat strangers. Hebrews 13 lets us know that some people throughout history were unaware that they had encounters with angels. No one knows when they shall appear. We do not know the physical condition, or shape of which God shall instruct the angel to adopt. It is important to connect spiritually with the message which the angel is communicating, because it is divine direction from God.

He will use angels to look after us when we cannot look after ourselves. It is this heavenly love which God intends to direct us until the day when He calls us home.

Let the Almighty bless you through the use of angels. Stay blessed.

D'Vinny

Day 21 | Success

"This book of the law shall not depart out of thy mouth; but thou shalt meditate therein day and night, that thou mayest observe to do according to all that is written therein: for then thou shalt make thy way prosperous, and then thou shalt have good success."

Joshua 1:8

The only real success is a saved soul that is granted entrance to heaven.

D'Vinny

No one starts his life, career, business, or other endeavor with the statement, "I want to be a failure." The desire for success is logical; no one aspires to be the next wino, drug addict, or person on skid row. Success is the natural objective of human effort.

King Solomon, the wisest man who had ever lived (see 1 Kings 3), repeatedly mentioned that it was all vanity and vexation of spirit (see Ecclesiastes 1 & 2). This wealthy educated king found that all accomplishments in life were shallow and meaningless unless man had a truly proper relationship with God. Human achievements—no matter of what importance—are meaningless without an understanding of Jesus Christ as our personal savior.

Success cannot be measured with physical things which are subject to the temporal limitation of this world. True success exists on a spiritual plane; wherein, the person knows accepts, loves, obeys, and worships God for himself. Earthly successes are not any good if the soul is lost and the person spends eternity outside the presence of God in a state of damnation.

Success through money, fame, popularity, and publicity will not allow one to have a good night's sleep or enjoy the value of true friendship. Success and its definition must be reshaped and recalibrated beyond the headlines of the front page of the newspaper.

The truth must be known: *only God can define and set the standards for success.* This formula is found repeatedly throughout the world's bestselling book, the Bible. There can be no success outside the will of God. If God is not a part of the adventure, then the Christian should not be either. God, through His Son, Jesus, is success. Spiritual success never fully materializes during life; it is realized at the final resting place of the soul.

Admission to heaven is the greatest success. Stay blessed.

D'Vinny

Day 22 | Mentorship

"Teaching us that, denying ungodliness and worldly lusts, we should live soberly, righteously, and godly, in this present world."

Titus 2:12

We must accept and follow the mentorship as given by the Holy Spirit of God.

D'Vinny

There is a quotation which states: "If you ever see a turtle on top of a telephone pole, you know that the turtle did not get there by himself." There is also the myth that a person is a "born leader" or "self-made" via some "Midas Touch." This flattery maybe a nice complement—when it is used appropriately—however, it is usually far from accurate.

Leadership, organizational, and entrepreneurial skills are the keys to these people. Sometimes people regard these abilities as innate, but regardless of aptitude or talent in a certain area it is important to realize that the talent has to be cultivated at some point. Without cultivation, the talent will remain in an underdeveloped state, not fully reaching its optimum potential. Herein, lies the job of a mentor.

A mentor is a special type of guide who is willing to impart knowledge and experience upon someone with potential. Mentorship requires two important components: The senior experienced person has to avail himself to provide the coaching, leadership, and encouragement to be bestowed upon the protégée. Likewise, the protégée needs to be willing to listen, learn, ascertain, and comprehend the subject matter at hand.

53

During the 2000 Summer Olympics, two sisters, Venus and Serena Williams, easily defeated their opponents from the Netherlands for the gold medal in women's doubles tennis. Although both were talented individual players, their success was largely due to their coaches, Billie Jean King and Zina Garrison. Both Williams sisters followed the mentorship and guidance of their coaches in order to achieve victory.

In the Old Testament, Elijah the Prophet mentored his understudy, Elisha. When Elijah left the earth for heaven on a chariot of fire, the spirit of Elijah rested upon Elisha (see II Kings 2). Likewise, in the New Testament the Apostle Paul mentored his young ministerial student Timothy who became an outstanding preacher of the Gospel.

It is the mentor's job to ensure that his talents, methodologies, and skills do not end with him. Effective mentors will always leave behind a legacy. It is only through mentorship that the statesman is able to live after his earthly life has been completed. The mentor will live on in the lives of each person whom he productively conducts toward the glory of God.

Bless another person's life by being a great mentor; in so doing, God will bless you. Stay blessed.

D'Vinny

Day 23 | Leadership

"Therefore now go, lead the people unto the place of which I have spoken unto thee: behold, mine Angel shall go before thee . . ."

(Exodus 32:34)

The true measure of leadership is the ability to solve problems as guided by the hand of God.

D'Vinny

The terms *leadership* and *management* are often used interchangeably. There is some similarity between these two concepts; however, leadership is broader and deeper in both meaning and application. Great religious, military, and government officials have usually been referred to as great leaders rather than great managers.

Leaders tend to look at things that appear impossible and to develop a solution. An excellent case was the superior leadership actions of Lee A. Iacocca, former chairman of Chrysler. Mr. Iacocca averted corporate bankruptcy of the automobile manufacturer twice—once during the 1970s, and again in the 1980s. The first aversion was achieved by securing federal loans which were paid back early and with interest. This proved to be profitable for Chrysler. The second was accomplished through new innovations to the product, and by a CEO who communicated directly to America. Mr. Iacocca did his own commercials.

Both incidences required leadership rather than management. A manager would have shut down the business—which was consistently losing money—but a leader took the impossible and turned it into an unexpected, overwhelming success. Our society needs more leaders and fewer managers.

Leadership starts in the home. Parents have to lead their children by spending quality time with them. Today there are too many parents who have relegated themselves to being "cellphone managers" of their children—as opposed to true parents. Cellphone parents will give their child a phone and drop him off at the mall with instructions to call every two hours. This is not parenting.

A parent's job is to pay close attention to the child's behavior and to cultivate his character. A sit-down family meal at the dinner table is a better approach than distant communication through a cellphone.

God chose Moses to deliver the Hebrew people from Egyptian slavery. The events of Moses' life, his struggles and trials, are detailed within the books of Exodus, Numbers, Leviticus, and Deuteronomy. The steadfastness, faith, and conviction exemplified by Moses far exceeded mere managerial ability. Moses was a leader who believed in the power of God to see him through any situation. Therefore, without an army or any type of military support, Moses boldly went before Pharaoh to deliver God's message: "Let my people go" (see Exodus 5).

A manager would ask God for more resources to accomplish the task. A leader relies on the Word of God, knowing that God is too wise to make a mistake and too divine to fail.

Ask God for the blessing of leadership skills. Stay blessed.

D'Vinny

Day 24 | Alcohol

"And be not drunk with wine, wherein is excess; but be filled with the Spirit."

Ephesians 5:18

Alcohol is a socially accepted form of voluntary poisoning, which is consumed under the pretense of "pleasure.

D'Vinny

There is an angry beast upon the nation's landscape. It consumes money, time, energy, health, and the lives of the people who consume *it*. The beast is called by numerous names, and it can never be sated. Marriages, jobs, and relationships have all crumbled within its fatal grip. The beast is alcohol.

Alcohol is the catalyst of many social ills, as it impairs judgment. It has caused people to make decisions which they normally would not have made while sober. There is a saying: "There are no ugly people in the bar after 2:00 a.m." This unwise attitude has caused many people to contract the deadly HIV virus.

People do things when they are impaired which they normally would not do otherwise. Another example is the problem with drunk drivers. Many innocent people have been killed by someone who decided that they needed "one more for the road." The political action group Mothers Against Drunk Driving (MADD) does an excellent job of supporting bereaved mothers and other family members after an ill-fated drunk driving fatality. Also MADD has brought about a change in society's attitude toward this issue. Society now realizes that drunk driving is a problem, and that the status quo has to change for the greater cause of safety and social responsibility.

Being drunk is a sin against God, a state in which the small spirits have taken over and the Spirit of God has been suppressed. The fifth chapter of Galatians says that drunkenness is a work of the flesh and, as such, will prevent entrance into the kingdom of heaven. A person cannot drink their way to heaven, but they can certainly drink their way into hell—with liquor upon their breath.

Alcohol consumption is a personal vice which some people tend to elevate to the status of necessity. The truth is that alcohol is nothing more than an attractive nuisance which has long-term negative effects. The Bible teaches us: "Wine is a mocker; strong drink is raging and whosoever is deceived thereby is not wise" (Proverbs 20:1). This lets us know that alcohol is best when it is used for symbolic or lightly therapeutic purposes—but never as a lifestyle.

Can God bless people when they are tipsy? Stay blessed.

D'Vinny

Day 25 | Cursing

"But shun profane and vain babblings: for they will increase unto more ungodliness."

2 Timothy 2:16

Words represent the inner spirit of man.

D'Vinny

The spoken word is dynamic and dramatic—more so than written communication. This is because vocal intonation and body language convey additional meanings: urgency, emotion, force, authority.

Yet, speech is quite often debased by the use of vile language. Profanity or cursing is not an attribute of holiness. It is sinful to its core, and it comes from the demonic forces of negativity. A person whose speech is peppered with this corrosive acid is one who is void of positive self-control and understanding. Even during times of excitement, stress, or other states of percolated emotion, when a person loses control by swearing, he demonstrates a spiritual imbalance.

The spirit must always be in control of the flesh. It is the spirit, the godly part of us, which keeps us focused on and connected to God. Our use of words must be reflective of the God who created us. He gave clear guidelines in the Bible by saying, "Do not use My name in vain" (see Exodus 20). Certainly, the idea of improperly using God's name is wrong; God is holy and so is His name. Therefore, righteous respect must be given to the One known as I Am, and this is furthered by keeping all of our speech devoid of sinful expression.

Parents are held accountable for the language which is used in their households. Children and young adults who curse have typically learned how to do so at home. They emulate this type of behavior from their parents and other authority figures; thus, the sinful demon of cursing is passed down along the family continuum.

It is Satan who loves the sound of cursing. It should be kept at the forefront of our spiritual consciousness that no one will be cursing as they pass through the pearly gates of heaven.

Remain righteous by using the right speech. Stay blessed.

D'Vinny

Day 26 | Education

"For Ezra had prepared his heart to seek the law of the LORD, and to do it, and to teach in Israel statutes and judgments."

Ezra 7:10

We are rapidly becoming a knowledge-based society.

D'Vinny

God gave man the ability to think and reason. This is needed because human beings do not run very well, swim very well, or fly by natural means. It is only through superior brainpower, as given by God, that man is able to control his environment.

It is through the development of the mind that humanity is able to understand the world and to solve complex problems—and thus make life better for all. The utilization of fire, the invention of the wheel, the steam engine, the automobile, and the innovations of modern medicine all demonstrate this.

Education enables individuals to effectively participate in present-day society, to earn a living. But more importantly education is needed for a person to be able to read, analyze, and comprehend the Word of God. While the Holy Bible is the world's bestselling book—found in most people's homes—not everyone around the world has the opportunity to become literate. Those with an education, especially a higher education, need to thank God for this blessing.

It is important to comprehend that some children have multiple strikes against them even before they step foot on a school campus. Students who come from an environment of poverty, unemployed parents, poor health care, and unstable households have a harder time than the more advantaged. Education, as represented by the wide range of local school systems across the world, has its challenges. There are a number of reforms which are being implemented throughout various parts of the United States, but it is teachers who can enact change on the individual level. They must have the ability to show love and concern, to teach beyond the landscape of socioeconomic disparity from which our children emerge. This challenge is not insurmountable; it can be done. A good teacher's personality is a gift from God. Greater is he who is in you than he who is in the world.

Education of our society will never be perfect; notwithstanding, education needs to be effective in order to allow a society to achieve the skills it needs to earn a living, and to read with joy the Word of God. Education will reveal that the scriptures are more than religious persuasions. The scriptures are actually spiritual nourishment for the soul—the Godly part within us.

The opportunity to get an education is a blessing from God. Stay blessed.

D'Vinny

Day 27 | Forgiveness

"For if ye forgive men their trespasses, your heavenly Father will also forgive you:"

Matthew 6:14

The act of forgiveness brings us more at one with God.

D'Vinny

Revenge is negative. It is a self-imposed judgment against another person. Typically, once a wronging takes place, the victim has a desire for some form of punishment against the perpetrator—payback. It is a misinterpretation of the "eye for an eye, tooth for a tooth" philosophy, as stated in the Old Testament (Exodus 21:24). This is one of the most abused passages of The Bible. The misapplication of this scripture will leave a person with one eye, a few teeth, and disfigured.

One of the greatest Christian attributes is practiced with limited frequency because of the human tendency to seek revenge for an injustice. Forgiveness is a beautiful characteristic of God. It takes love. It takes self-discipline and self-control in order to keep forgiveness in one's heart. One of the reasons why the divorce rate is so high in the United States is due to a lack of forgiveness by one or both spouses. Neither human being in the marriage is perfect; both parties will make mistakes. Forgiveness is a medicine from God which has instant healing power.

Forgiveness is healthy because it is a great reliever of stress. The enormous pressure of resentment is sometimes worse than the pain of the original infraction. Headaches, high blood pressure, loss of sleep and appetite, and other physiological problems can be mitigated through a prescription of God's medicine of forgiveness.

Moreover, it is important to realize that forgiveness is a requirement of God. God wants Christians to forgive, not only other Christians, but everyone for their transgressions (see Mark 11). Jesus, the Son of God, taught His disciples how to pray what is known as the Lord's Prayer (see Matthew 6). The supplicatory phrase "and forgive us our debts, as we forgive our debtors" is found in this prayer. We are asking God to forgive us, just as we forgive our fellow man. If our neighbors do not deserve forgiveness, how can we expect it ourselves?

Practice the principle of forgiveness and watch the blessings from God increase. Stay blessed.

D'Vinny

Day 28 | Meekness

"Seek ye the LORD, all ye meek of the earth, which have wrought his judgment; seek righteousness, seek meekness: it may be ye shall be hid in the day of the LORD's anger."

Zephaniah 2:3

Meekness builds character like no other attribute.

D'Vinny

Contemporary society inaccurately associates meekness with weakness, because the world has taught us to be cynical. Some philosophies of today are: "Let no one get the best of you," "Always stand your ground," and "Winning is the only worthy outcome." These are self-centered displays of arrogance which are always destructive in the end.

Attempts to be controlling, arrogant, and revengeful lead to a dead-end. To be meek is to surrender the control of our lives over to God, who is loving and wise. A person may be ridiculed who follows the Holy Bible and tries to live right in accordance with godly teachings and direction. Nevertheless, God's way is the only way.

The Bible views meekness in a diametrically opposite position than the world does. Jesus' first recorded oration was His famous Sermon on the Mount. He began with a preamble known as "The Beatitudes," the purpose of which was to inform humanity how to be blessed by God and to achieve the profound state of happiness. Beatitudes means "blessed," which in turn means "happiness." The quality is held in paramount regard throughout The Bible. Jesus even referred to Himself as "meek and lowly in heart" (Matthew 11:29).

Meekness implies having our individual spirit in tune with God's, in order to achieve a peacefulness of mind. It takes forgiveness and a penitent humility in order to be meek. It is not weakness; it is the coalescence of all Christian attributes, applicable most when we make tough decisions—our ethics on the table.

Meekness is not something that one does. It is a spiritual state which is best arrived at through prayer and obedience to God. The Lord loves us, and He blesses those who serve Him by displaying the Godly characteristic of meekness; for it leads to peace with God and the continued rejoicing and celebration when we shall join God, spirit-to-spirit.

May your blessings from heaven increase as you seek the quality of meekness. Stay blessed.

D'Vinny

Day 29 | Hope

"And have hope toward God . . ."

Acts 24:15a

Without hope how can good things happen?

D'Vinny

Hope is based upon the premise that, regardless of the current circumstances, the future will be brighter than the past and the present. Hope is positive projection upon the days to come. It gives us the courage and inspiration to endure the temporary hardships of life, knowing that one day change will come.

Job is an excellent example of one who was rich and lost everything. He lost all ten of his children to a traumatic windstorm, possibly a tornado, which took all their lives instantaneously. Most parents today would require a tranquilizer to make it through that kind of ten-casket funeral. We expect our children to bury us. Nevertheless, Job was able to persevere, to continue onward, because he knew that God would bring him through this most difficult situation.

He kept this positive attitude even when sickness entered his own body. Steadfastly, Job maintained hope, knowing that God was the One who was in charge and in control of both life and death.

One of the central themes of the civil rights leader and Baptist minister Rev. Jesse Jackson is to "keep hope alive." Without hope, an individual self-destruct. The same goes for the family, neighborhood, city, and state. We need this optimistic mentality to guide us through our hardships. It is most important to remember that the future is in God's Hands, because it belongs to Him. Consequently, only He has the answer.

Our greatest hope is not earthly; it is not physical. It is spiritual, centered around Jesus, the savior of the world. The Son of God will never disappoint us. Once we are spiritually connected to Christ, our earthly situations—no matter how difficult they seem at times—will become bearable. We will say with a strong declaration of faith, "It was The Lord who saved me and brought me through the fire of life as a testimony and praise to His Glory."

Hope in Jesus Christ Our Lord brings the blessings of God. Stay blessed.

D'Vinny

Day 30 | Worship

"Sanctify ye a fast, call a solemn assembly, gather the elders and all the inhabitants of the land into the house of the LORD your God, and cry unto the LORD."

Joel 1:14

A person's life is incomplete without proper worship unto God.

D'Vinny

The body consists of three major components: There is the biological part, the physical body. There is the spirit, or godly part. Finally, there is the soul. These three components can be better understood by contemplating the moment of death. When this occurs, both the spirit and the soul depart from the deceased. The spirit always goes back to God (see Ecclesiastes 12), and the body goes to the earth from whence it was created (see Genesis 3). The soul goes to heaven or hell, depending upon one's relationship with God through His Son, Jesus.

During the earthly existence known as life, we have a desire to worship. Man has an internal drive to connect himself to something. Often times, if people are not trained well, they will worship their job, house, social status, financial accumulation, leisure time, sleep, adventure—the list continues *ad nauseam.*

The sports person who, on the morning of the Sabbath, totally disregards God yet religiously never misses the big game is a sports worshipper. Being a sports fan is his number one priority. On the opening kickoff, if his team receives the ball from deep within their own end zone, and they make an unexpected, spectacular return for a gaming-winning touchdown, the fan will cheer and shout.

The car buff who uses the Sabbath to wash one or more of his cars is actually worshipping them. He is placing them ahead of the time which is allocated for worshipping God. The car becomes an idol (see Exodus 20). The person takes time to bend down to wash the tires. This is bowing down to his idol. The person is using hand and arm motions to wash and wax the car; this is praise to the idol. One of the offerings that was required in the Old Testament was a wave offering to God (see Exodus 29, & Leviticus 7).

It would be great if the car were put in its proper place by being washed the day before, and then driven to church on the Sabbath; it would aid the owner in his worship to God instead of the opposite.

Whatever a person puts first in his life is his god, and it shall become the thing that he will worship. The issue is what will he choose? Will the person worship the One who created him? Is there a longing of the soul and spirit of the created to have love for his Creator? Indeed, man was made to worship. The true question for each individual is who or what?

Worship God on earth and experience the blessing of heaven. Stay blessed.

D'Vinny

Day 31 | Negotiation

"If my people, which are called by my name, shall humble themselves, and pray, and seek my face, and turn from their wicked ways; then will I hear from heaven, and will forgive their sin, and will heal their land."

2 Chronicles 7:14

All human interaction concerns itself with some form of negotiation.

D'Vinny

The act of negotiating is often viewed as a contest of wit which involves complex maneuvering and gamesmanship. True negotiations have a godly humanitarian focus on placing the needs of others before the needs of oneself. It works best when both sides win. Therefore, in true effective negotiations there is no loser. A long-term relationship of mutual respect is forged when both sides have achieved equilibrium.

The number one problem with negotiation is sin. There are typically, though not exclusively, three common types: The first is the transmission of pride, wherein, someone always wants to reign superior by being the "top dog" with the loudest bark. This is the person or group of people who will quickly announce that he is in charge of the talks. The next is lying, when one will simply not tell the truth. He comes packed with lies— the PowerPoint charts, histograms, financial projections, risk analysis—these documents are often times deceptive. The third sin is greed. The desire to get the most money in the quickest manner becomes a poison that infects the righteous conscience of many.

All quick profits are not good profits. Oliver Stone, the movie producer, was not right in his film, *Wall Street*: ". . . greed is good, greed is right, greed is what made this country great." The truth is greed is sin, and it is a type of behavior which does not please God.

Both sides must come to the table with something to offer. All individuals must be able to comprehend how to help the other solve his problem and achieve success. More importantly, all those involved must invite God and the presence of His Holy Spirit to be a part of the negotiation process so that God's wisdom can manifest itself.

It is important to remember that negotiations must always involve the Spirit of God. Only He can successfully bless both sides with fairness, honesty, and long-term success.

Include God in all negotiations and receive heavens results. Stay blessed.

D'Vinny

Day 32 | Landmines

"Thou shalt not kill."

Deuteronomy 5:17

Landmines are man's misuse of the earth, which is an extreme insult to God.

D'Vinny

There is an evil of indiscriminate killing that occurs around the world. This killer does not care whether its victims are soldiers, noncombatant civilians, children, or animals. An innocent bird that happens to be soaring through the air might stop on the ground to get a worm, but when it attempts to take off and the pressure is released, *ka-boom.*

Landmines are the most insensitive killers on the planet. Anything that unfortunately strays into a minefield is subject to this nefarious terror. These are evil devices that represent an absence of humanity and a total disregard for the God-given environment.

A soldier with a rifle can make a judgment call as to whether a potential target should be engaged. Humans can reason that not everyone who is in a combat zone is a target. This is especially true toward fighting done in cities and villages. Most nations, when engaged in warfare, try to avoid as much collateral damage as possible, because people have to attempt to go back to some form of a normal life at the end of the conflict.

Warfare gets out of control when landmines are used. These devices can turn a vegetable garden capable of feeding entire families and neighborhoods into an instant cemetery. Instead of producing life-sustaining, beautiful vegetables, the land will now produce dead bodies and amputated body parts.

Landmines can never justified. God will not accept any form or rationalization of their usage from any nation on earth. God is not pleased by this misuse of His land which He gave to Adam and his descendants. He instructed them to be caretakers of the earth (see Genesis 2). God did not make the soil to be used in this manner of evil, and man, in all of his endeavors and activities, is accountable to the Lord. It is the will of God that should always govern humanity.

Worldwide removal of landmines would be a great blessing to humanity. Stay blessed.

D'Vinny

Day 33 | Words

"And the LORD answered the angel that talked with me with good words and comfortable words."

Zechariah 1:13

Words represent the inner spirit of a person.

D'Vinny

The spoken word is a powerful form of communication. Pitch, volume, tone, rate of speed, and inflection all serve to make our speech more dynamic. But what is important to examine are the words which we use.

Negative words can destroy an individual's self-esteem, especially when he directs the comment inward toward his own mental psyche. Consider the following examples of phrases which have a negative impact:

"Boy, you are worthless."

"You couldn't think your way out of a wet paper bag."

"You will never amount to anything."

"You are not smart enough."

"You are just an average plain Jane; you are not beautiful enough."

The list is endless. These sayings deduct value from a person, who is in fact a child of God. They can leave internal scars which are difficult to heal. Each of us must bridle our tongues. We must think before we speak. The spirit must be engaged before the mouth is put into motion. This is vitally important, because whatever is inside of the speaker will come out in his words.

A Christian must be careful not to use any type of speech that would dishonor God, but rather to utilize kind speech which is pleasing unto God. Kind speech is peaceful, respectful, and it is one of the greatest methods in achieving diplomatic success in a difficult situation.

Our words can be long-lasting and take permanent hold for ages to come. Consider, "Ask not what your country can do for you, but what you can do for your country," and, "I have a dream." These are words which have inspired generations, and they will be around for a very long time on the landscape of American social consciousness.

The most meaningful of words are found in the scriptures, which represent the Word of God. Let the Holy Spirit, by use of the scriptures, guide our tongues, control our words so that we will not cause pain. May our speech always pay tribute to God.

Glorify God in your speech and He shall glorify you with His blessings. Stay blessed.

D'Vinny

Day 34 | Superpower

"Daniel answered and said, Blessed be the name of God for ever and ever: for wisdom and might are his: And he changeth the times and the seasons: he removeth kings, and setteth up kings: he giveth wisdom unto the wise, and knowledge to them that know understanding."

Daniel 2:20-21

Arrogant pride often precedes the fall of once-great nations.

D'Vinny

The term "superpower" has been frequently used to refer to nations who have achieved a state of great military and economic importance. During the Cold War, the United States and the Soviet Union were considered to be the two most dominant superpowers in the world. After the fall of the Berlin Wall and the dissolution of the USSR, the United States was left as the most influential superpower in the world. This has placed enormous responsibility upon the United States. The old Cold War system of checks and balances on an international level is no longer in force, and the US has more pressure to self-govern itself.

The concept of "sole superpower" is a misguided one which yields a false sense of superiority. If it is taken for granted, it will quickly lead us down the highway of arrogance to a place of sinful indifference toward the rest of the world. This attitude can also lead to a false sense of security, which, as we have seen, can be quickly shattered by potential enemies who desire to perpetuate violence and destruction.

The question has been asked throughout history: "Where does evil come from?" It should be viewed in a righteous context in order to fully ascertain its characteristics. Expressed simply, evil is sin, and sin always exists where it is least expected. Thus, the best way to understand evil is for each individual nation to ensure that it is right with God. The secondary thing is to ensure that it is right with its neighbors.

No single nation, from the greatest on earth to the poorest, can be successful without the presence and blessings of the Hand of God. It is He who created all nations. God through His Spirit has allowed the various events in human history to draw the international borders. Any superpower, both now and in the future, must humble itself before God and be willing to be a servant to all His people.

God is the only true superpower; all other superpowers are false gods. Stay blessed.

D'Vinny

Day 35 | Decisions

"And Elijah came unto all the people, and said, How long halt ye between two opinions? if the LORD be God, follow him: but if Baal, then follow him. And the people answered him not a word."

1 Kings 18:21

The essence of life is effective decision making as led by God.

D'Vinny

Each difficult issue in life is ultimately resolved by a making a decision. A teenager who is graduating from high school has a variety of options. A choice has to be made based on the interests, desires, and future aspirations of the graduate. Some enter the workforce right away, others join the military or head off to an institution of higher education. It is important to make a decision and put forth the best effort to build a life that will be pleasing unto God. Yet, many do nothing. They let time pass as if they were a deer in headlights, immobilized. This indecisiveness is the *refusal* to make a decision.

Similarly, one of the worst things that can manifest within a romantic relationship is a fear of commitment. For many years the boyfriend and girlfriend are stuck in the same rut, trying to figure out if they are right for each other. If people have been dating for a long time and nothing happens in the form of marriage, then it is time to break up and seek opportunities elsewhere. The legendary singer Diana Ross sang these words in a Motown release: "You don't really love me / you just keep me hangin' on." This concept of "indecisive immobilization" is real, and lives are wasted as a result. God will never bless the relationship until it has been consummated by marriage.

God expects all of us to make a decision concerning our spiritual nature. Joshua in his farewell address to the Hebrew nation reminded people that God was responsible for their deliverance. He charged the people with the responsibility to make a decision as to which god they would serve (see Joshua 24). Likewise, in 1 Kings 18, on Mount Carmel, Elijah asked the people, "How long halt ye between two opinions? If the LORD be God, follow him: but if Baal, then follow him." The immediate reaction was that of indecisive immobilization. The Bible records in that same chapter: ". . . and the people answered him not a word."

Jesus wanted a decision from Peter when he asked, "Whom do men say that I am?" Then Jesus asked Peter an important question, one which each of us has to answer today: "Whom do you say I am?" The worst thing Peter could have said was, "I don't know. I'm still trying to figure it out; catch me later." This would have been indecisive immobilization. Instead, Peter answered in the affirmative, as guided by the Holy Spirit of God, "You are the Christ, Son of the Living God" (Matthew 16).

Life is about decisions. Each of us will either be a failure or a success based on the choices we make. May God through His Spirit be present in our lives when we make life-altering decisions.

God blesses righteous decision making. Stay blessed.

D'Vinny

Day 36 | Inspiration

"But there is a spirit in man: and the inspiration of the Almighty giveth them understanding."

Job 32:8

True inspiration comes from God.

D'Vinny

No one is completely independent. Each of us will get weary on our journey through life. Every day is not filled with warm rays of sunshine and great joy. Sometimes things occur which can cause a setback in our plans. A neighborhood fire, an accident or unexpected illness—indeed, life is filled with many troubles we must encounter.

There is a human tendency to absorb a catastrophic calamity or a series of consecutive mini problems with a certain level of strength and fortitude. However, our inspiration comes from the One who created us. All situations, whether they are good or bad, are under the control of God. Proverbs, the Bible's book of wisdom, teaches: "The Lord hath made all things for himself yea, even the wicked for the day of evil" (Proverbs 16:4).

The knowledge that God, through the guidance of His Word and through His compassion, love, and mercy as demonstrated by His Son, Jesus, is all that we need to inspire us to go through any situation in life. It is important to realize when we wake up each morning that God has a plan for us—even for that specific day. The very fact that we are here means that God sees value for us on earth, and that His purpose for us has not yet been fulfilled. When God is finished with us, then He calls the saved souls to heaven. An unsaved or condemned soul will be called at the time of death to a place away from the presence of God. True inspiration is derived from the knowledge of our final place, where we shall spend eternity.

Let us not become sidetracked by depressing earthly situations, whether it be the bitterness of divorce, financial difficulty, health issues, or any other problems which Satan may place in our way. Our love for God and His Love for us is our inspiration. May each of us find a perfect peace with our Maker.

The blessings of God are inspiration for a lifetime. Stay blessed.

D'Vinny

Day 37 | Justice

*"But let judgment run down as waters, and righteous-
ness as a mighty stream."*

Amos 5:24

*The justice of man should be based upon the righteous-
ness of God.*

D'Vinny

The concept of justice—be it within a family, religious group, state, or nation—is based upon the particu-
lar values of that enclave and is directly dependent upon
one's proximity with God or one's proximity with Satan. God's Hand is upon a just society. This is a community in which the application of justice is unbiased
and fair.

A judicial system must be rooted in a fairness and
impartiality, showing no favoritism. Unfortunately, so-
cio-economic conditions have often tilted the scales by
way of partial treatment from law enforcement, judges,
and jurors. Race, education, status, and social influence
should not carry more weight than the evidence or the
testimony of witnesses. The multi-millionaire athlete
must be treated the same as the homeless person.

Jesus is familiar with injustice, Himself being the
victim of a kangaroo court verdict. Jesus' trial consisted
of conflicting witnesses, a viscous prosecutor, incompe-
tent judges, and a fickle jury who praised him in the beginning yet wanted Him crucified by the end of the
week.

The Bible teaches what a witness is supposed to do.
The Son of God gave these instructions: "Verily, Verily,
I say unto thee, we speak that we do know and testify

that we have seen" (see John 3). Every witness is actually an employee of God when they are on the stand giving a testimony. God demands on the truth.

God, through His Son, Jesus, understands the problems of a lack of societal justice. The Creator of mankind will be the final judge and the ultimate administrator of justice.

God's blessings are the purest form of justice. Stay blessed.

D'Vinny

Day 38 | Faith

"Now faith is the substance of things hoped for, the evidence of things not seen."

Hebrews 11:1

Faith is man's reliance on the Holy Spirit of God for direction.

D'Vinny

There is a natural tendency for people to try to figure things out for themselves. This premise is one of the foundations of the academic educational system, especially in the scientific and mathematical realms. We are taught to develop critical thinking skills in a variety of disciplines, to have the ability to solve complex problems and understand their impact upon the human condition. If there is a federal budget deficit, we use macroeconomics to find a solution. If there is a problem with an infectious disease, we turn to biology and chemistry.

Similarly, we like to see things "with our own eyes." Yet man cannot see God, physically. This is the reason why many people do not believe in God. Faith uses the vision of the Holy Spirit. Mathematically, faith is 0% dependent on man and 100% dependent on God. Faith requires the giving up of self and the ability to trust and believe in the One who said, "Let there be light" (see Genesis 1). Immediately light came into existence upon hearing and obeying the sound of God's voice.

God has not changed. He is the same, always and forever. Of us, He requires the profession and application of faith, so that our spirit can connect with God's Holy Spirit. "But without faith it is impossible to please him: for he that cometh to God must believe that he is, and that he is a rewarder of them that diligently seek him" (Hebrews 11:6).

Faith is an internal condition which is an affirmation of external possibility. When friends turn away, when a situation goes from dim to dark, from bad to worse, when hope is almost gone, God can step in and do what seems impossible. He is, after all, a miracle-working God. If there is no faith, there is no spiritual power. Physical power always fails at some point, but faith in God never fails, because heaven is the ultimate reward for the faithful.

Faithfulness to God brings untold blessings. Stay blessed.

D'Vinny

Day 39 | War

"And he shall judge among many people, and rebuke strong nations afar off; and they shall beat their swords into plowshares, and their spears into pruninghooks: nation shall not lift up a sword against nation, neither shall they learn war anymore."

Micah 4:3

Nations who look to start war do not honor God.

D'Vinny

Man is God's greatest creation on earth, made in His image. It is therefore difficult to understand why this highly intelligent lifeform has a recurring problem of mass, organized killing. Unfortunately, war has been a regular event throughout human history. The categorization of eras has often been defined by periods of war, the outcomes of which have redrawn international borders and changed political regimes.

Warfare is a consequence of regional, national, and international politics. It is a total breakdown in the negotiation process of diplomacy. Many nations believe that there is a peace to be achieved on the other side of warfare. If this were the case, there would not have been a war fought after World War I, which was known as the "Great War."

The act of war very rarely solves problems. It simply rearranges pieces on the human chess board of understanding. Human behavior has not changed in thousands of years. People, even generations later still possess the same elements of human frailty; put succinctly, people are still people.

The reality is that the true winner in warfare, always and forever, shall be the cemetery. It is the grave which collects the fallen bodies from both sides of the conflict. Regardless of the outcome between the opposing military forces, in the spiritual sense the winner never achieves a total victory. One war sets the conditions for the next war; whether it is ten, fifty, or one hundred years in the future.

All wars are avoidable. An element of sin, known as hatred, is often present when a nation decides to use force. It is difficult to engage in war when God is given the glory and honor, He deserves. It is especially difficult to shed blood when love is expressed in a Godly manner toward others. Whenever war is declared, there is an absence of Godly love between neighbors.

Use of non-militaristic methods will help us to avoid armed conflict, especially when a situation is given over to God and placed under the guidance of the Holy Spirit. Man must let the Creator—not warfare—reign supreme.

All national leaders should march to the tune of the wisdom of God—not the drums of war. Stay blessed.

D'Vinny

Day 40 | Thankfulness

"I thank my God, making mention of thee always in my prayers."

Philemon 1:4

God expects thankfulness and praise from us.

D'Vinny

Thankfulness is an expression of sincere appreciation for an act of kindness or mercy which was rendered. The person who is giving thanks is demonstrating respectful Christian character with an act of humility and obedience toward God. It helps to remind ourselves of the importance of the commandment given by Christ: ". . . Thou shalt love thy neighbor as thyself" (see Matthew 19).

One of the best ways to fully comprehend the importance of thankfulness is to observe the converse within our society. There is sadness in the phrase: "Look what I did for myself." Part of humanity is lost because many are focused on the big three of self: Me, Myself, and I. Another problem is the overuse of the phrase: "I got lucky." The reality is that there is no such thing as luck. Proper thanks should be rendered to God, the One who delivers blessings in our lives. God does not use luck; He uses blessings, and He works miracles. A Christian should eradicate the word "luck" from his vocabulary and instead give thanks unto God upon the receipt of a blessing.

True thankfulness is a condition of the heart. Gratitude connects man with his fellow man—and with God. Often times, God will work through one person to bless another. Evidence of this is given daily, such as in the

89

scenario of an automobile accident. A pedestrian who witnesses a horrific accident will be touched by God to call 911 or perform CPR until proper emergency care arrives. Frequently, it is the medical aid which is given in the first ten to fifteen minutes that will determine if the victim lives or dies. If a patient has lost too much blood from a wound and vital, then chances of recovery are slim. But we often see that God will send a bystander who knows how to apply a tourniquet, giving the situation a much different outcome.

God is the one who deserves our praise. Thanks, should be given for the small things as well as the big things that He has done for us.

Our appreciation of God brings more blessings. Stay blessed.

D'Vinny

Day 41 | God

"The LORD is good, a strong hold in the day of trouble; and he knoweth them that trust in him."

Nahum 1:7

"The fool hath said in his heart, there is no God. They are corrupt, they have done abominable works, there is none that doeth good."

Psalms 14:1

An atheist does not understand that he is inextricably linked to God.

D'Vinny

God is the Supreme Being. He is the creator of the earth as well as the rest of the universe. God has always existed—before time, light, and space were conceived.

He is often referred to as the Holy Trinity or the Triune God because God is a composite of three spiritual beings: the Father, the Son, and the Holy Spirit. Each part of the Holy Trinity is masculine and should never be referred to by otherwise. The correct pronouns are "He" and "Him," and even these should be used sparingly when referencing God. Moreover, the Holy Spirit should never be referred as "It"; the Holy Spirit is "He".

God is holy. God is divine. God is love. God should always be respected, revered, and obeyed by man. God is everything that man needs before man even knows he needs it.

The reason why some people do not believe that God exists is because they are trying to analyze God from a physical standpoint. God is a spirit (see John 4). When people try to apply their five senses to experience

God, they do not understand that God is metaphysical, and they always come up short. Nevertheless, many people still try to use the physical approach; they want to see God, hear God, touch God. Given that He is intangible, the only methods to apply are faith and obedience.

Ultimately this question will be answered at the time of death, once our soul has separated from the body. We shall meet God and be granted a final resting place—either with Him in heaven—or in hell, a place of torment and agony away from God. There will not be time to develop a belief in God after one's life has run out. At that point, it will be too late.

Knowing and loving God is the world's greatest blessing. Stay blessed.

D'Vinny

Day 42 | Poverty

"For ye know the grace of our Lord Jesus Christ, that, though he was rich, yet for your sakes he became poor, that ye through his poverty might be rich."

2 Corinthians 8:9

Spiritual poverty is a greater concern than financial poverty; gain spiritual riches through love.

D'Vinny

No one has "being poor" on his to-do list. Unfortunately, it is an unpleasant reality for approximately one-third of the world's population. Poverty exists for many reasons: war, famine, disease, corruption, illiteracy, overpopulation, crime, natural disaster—the list goes on, and many people who are born poor never break the cycle as a result of self-marginalization.

Jesus mentioned during Passion Week, His last days on earth, that we would always have the poor among us. This divine proclamation means that, despite all effort exerted on the individual and governmental level, we will never completely eradicate poverty from the world. But there is also a Christian requirement to provide assistance to the poor: "We then that are strong ought to bear the infirmities of the weak, and not to please ourselves" (Romans 15:1).

Most industrialized nations have attempted to structure their economies so that the poorest will still have an acceptable minimum standard of living. Ideally, as the economy improves over time, this minimum standard is raised, the goal being that poverty within industrialized nations does not have to mean homelessness and starvation. Basic subsistence should be guaranteed through federal or state funding, as well as through private philanthropy.

One effective way to reduce poverty abroad, particularly in the least-developed countries, is through the use of micro-loans, which are typically for less than a thousand dollars. This financial tool enables people to start their own businesses without fear of incurring an intimidating amount of debt and is small enough to be paid back over time without excessive charges or fees. It is a means of obtaining working capital which allows purchase of the tools and materials necessary to get a business started. Thus, people are able to create more opportunities for themselves, their families, and their communities.

At the local level, working toward reducing crime and political corruption, increasing opportunities for education, and helping people develop job skills will provide the disadvantaged with a greater chance for success. A stable government is paramount to a society moving forward.

All of the above remedies are important in the effort to diminish poverty, but the absolute greatest course of action is *philos*, or brotherly love. This love is the sharing of resources among nations, allowing this world to become a true brotherhood. Love is a public policy that will never fail. Love represents God, because God is love (see 1 John 4).

By helping those less fortunate we receive the blessings of God. Stay blessed.

D'Vinny

Day 43 | Homelessness

"And Jesus said unto him, Foxes have holes, and birds of the air have nests; but the Son of man hath not where to lay his head."

Luke 9:58

The condition of homelessness only applies to earth; no one will be homeless in heaven.

D'Vinny

The economic status of an individual will not always remain constant. Economic conditions can and will change over the course of time. Likewise, in both good and bad times, money does not always trickle down to the lowest echelon of the working class— meaning that the poor do not always get the crumbs from the rich man's table.

Sometimes people can be removed from a lofty economic status within a short period of time. A real estate crash or a plunge in the stock market can have a devastating impact upon one's standard of living, leading to repossession, bankruptcy, or foreclosure on one's home. One of the worst situations a person can have to deal with is to lose the roof over his head, moving from stabilization to destitution. The recent mortgage crisis is evidence of this, as well as Hurricanes Katrina, Andrew, Camille—as well as other natural disasters that have managed to put rich people, middle-class people, and poor people into the same instantaneous category— homeless.

This is an issue which requires attention at all levels. Effective policies have to be put into place in order to reduce the number of homeless people. Education, job training, adult literacy programs, and drug rehabilitation are methods with which success has been achieved. It is not someone else's problem—it is a problem for society as a whole.

Jesus understands the homeless. He was born into poverty and temporary homelessness in the town of Bethlehem. Furthermore, Jesus was homeless during His forty days in the wilderness. Later, He made a proclamation about His condition: "Foxes have holes, and birds of the air have nests; but the Son of man hath not where to lay his head."

No matter what the specific causes of homelessness are, God expects positive action based on love for thy neighbor to address the problem—and for God's Spirit to be present.

The blessings of God can overcome any condition. Stay blessed.

D'Vinny

Day 44 | Honesty

"Finally, brethren, whatsoever things are true, whatsoever things are honest, whatsoever things are just, whatsoever things are pure, whatsoever things are lovely, whatsoever things are of good report; if there be any virtue, and if there be any praise, think on these things."
Philippians 4:8

The power of the honest word is often overlooked.
D'Vinny

Honesty is the ability to tell the truth in a complete, accurate, and straightforward manner. This concept of pure communication appears to be disappearing from today's society. Often times a person's words have to be closely examined to ascertain the facts and true intention.

A person's word is his bond. The information which a person provides is a reflection of his innermost character. Clearly, the antithesis of honesty is dishonesty. They cannot occupy the same space at the same time. Light and darkness cannot coexist; they are polar opposites of each other.

One of the reasons why the divorce rate is over 50% in the United States is because of dishonesty. Some people enter into a marriage and still want to be single. They never give up the single mentality or lifestyle. They become dishonest in their finances by spending on pleasure and recreation first, as opposed to their responsibilities. Likewise, outside relationships—an extreme form of dishonesty—have caused the termination of many marriages.

The spiritual principle of honesty should be followed at all times. Honesty is a reflection of the mindset of God, whereas dishonesty is a manifestation of Satan. Deception and lies cannot stand the test of time. During the trial regarding the sinking of the Titanic, the crew testified that the ship went down whole and sank in one piece. The surviving passengers said that the ship broke into two pieces as it was sinking. The court chose to believe the crew and take the opinion that the ship went down like a lady. Decades later, with improved technology, the Atlantic Ocean revealed the truth in two pieces on its dark, muddy floor. Consequently, history corrected itself and the truth was revealed.

The most important aspect of honesty is where each person stands in their relationship with his Creator. Dishonesty separates a person's soul from God. Honesty, with the objective of getting right with God and living righteously in His eyes, results in a favorable outcome when each of us will see Him on the other side.

Honesty in the most difficult times brings about the blessings of God. Stay blessed.

D'Vinny

Day 45 | Family

"And that these days should be remembered and kept throughout every generation, every family, every province, and every city . . ."

Esther 9:28a

God established the family before He established the Church.

D'Vinny

The nucleus of any conglomeration of people—be it a community, city, state, church, or nation—is predicated upon the condition of the families within it. God has properly designed the family. It starts with the marriage between a man and a woman, with the male figure accountable, as husband and father, for the family's well-being. Whenever God's plan is altered by man's ungodly desires, such as marriage alternatives, abuse, etc., then the family suffers.

As a result, so does society. Every day the education system receives our children, the products of our families. Functional families send children to school who have had a good dinner the previous evening, a full night's rest, and breakfast before they arrive at school. These children will have on clean clothes and will have been taught the importance of showing respect for those in authority, as well as respect for their fellow students. These children are prepared to get a solid education.

Conversely, dysfunctional families who have problems with providing their children with a basic level of support—such as food, clothing, shelter, and healthcare—facilitate an uphill battle for their children. This is compounded when parents don't check homework, are not involved, or have an indifferent attitude toward the value of an education.

Likewise, the legal system receives them. The policemen, as they are putting handcuffs on a teenager, should not be the first to impose ethics and the difference between right and wrong—that is the job of the family. God expects the family to first be accountable to Him, to teach the children His standards. God determines which behaviors and values are acceptable and holy, and likewise it is He who determines which ones are sinful; this should be taught from an early age.

The Holy Bible records the Ten Commandments as being the only scripture directly written by the Hand of God (see Exodus 20). All other scripture was written by man, under the direct guidance of the Holy Spirit. All laws and ordinances can be directly connected to the Ten Commandments because they are the foundation of good human behavior, and God expects His guidelines to be taught and obeyed within the family—and, subsequently, by society.

The culminating point on which to reflect is that God created the family, and He will hold the family accountable to Him. God created the family before the church because it is the most integral aspect of all society.

Strengthen your family and enjoy the blessings of God. Stay blessed.

D'Vinny

Day 46 | Materialism

"Ye have sown much, and bring in little; ye eat, but ye have not enough; ye drink, but ye are not filled with drink; ye clothe you, but there is none warm; and he that earneth wages earneth wages to put it into a bag with holes."

Haggai 1:6

High-rate interest on debt is a monthly thief that destroys the financial well-being of a person.

D'Vinny

We live in a society driven by consumerism. The economic objective of corporations is to increase sales growth and revenue. This requires consumers to increase their demand for various products and services in the marketplace. Quite frequently this demand is stimulated by new products; an example would be the invention and marketing of the cellular telephone. Sometimes demand is driven by the improvement of existing products.

But all materialism is not bad. A 35-year-old vehicle probably does not have the latest safety features, like anti-lock brakes, multiple airbags, or built-in GPS. Yet, it is important not to get engulfed in materialism for the sake of materialism. This form of consumption is closely associated with greed. The act of wanting something because it exists, whether or not the person has the ability to comfortably afford the item without financial strain, is without sound logic.

Creative financing through credit cards has been widely adopted as a viable method of purchasing—now being the preferred medium of exchange—but the misuse of credit has caused severe financial damage to many. Consider the sub-prime lending crisis of the late 2000s, an event that was caused by reckless mortgage financing, allowing people to buy expensive homes with no money down. Adjustable-rate mortgages extended people beyond their economical means. This led to an explosion of debt which has resulted in discomfort and despair.

Jesus understands the problems of materialism. Lucifer offered Him the kingdoms of this world, with no money down, no interest rate, no co-signer, and same-day immediate possession (see Matthew 4). Jesus refused because it was not God's purpose for His life. Our example of "success over materialism" is God's Son, Jesus.

A vast accumulation of material goods will never compare to the accumulation of character; let God develop one's character and the blessings shall unfold. Stay blessed.

D'Vinny

Day 47 | Mercy

"It is of the LORD's mercies that we are not consumed, because his compassions fail not. They are new every morning: great is thy faithfulness."

Lamentations 3:22-23

Mercy is a greater instrument than revenge or punishment.

D'Vinny

Two reactions are available toward one who trespasses against us: mercy or punishment. Mercy is an unmerited favor which is given to someone deserving of some form of punishment. A Christian principle that, when applied, is mutually beneficial to all parties involved, mercy is an act of love that emulates one of God's greatest character traits. It is an application of love, an act of kindness which is not earned by its recipient or required of its provider.

When mercy is given from God, is it His Divinity being bestowed upon humanity. When extended between human beings, it is a gracious form of humanitarianism as directed by the Holy Spirit.

Jesus, the Son of God, lived His entire life teaching mercy. It was an essential part of His character. It was in His heart. Jesus exemplified and answered the question of the Old Testament Prophet Micah: ". . . O man, what is good; and what doth the Lord require of thee, but to do justly and to love mercy, and to walk humbly with thy God?" (Micah 6:8).

Jesus gave many examples of mercy during His earthly ministry. The man who was blinded from birth received his eyesight by having a merciful encounter with Jesus (see John 9). The woman at the well who had multiple divorces and was living in a sinful state of co-habitation directly experienced a conversation of mercy with Jesus. Her resulting testimony to the town was: "Come see a man which told me all things that ever I did: is not this the Christ?" (John 4:29).

Jesus' last earthly act of mercy was on the cross. He showed love for His mother by placing her in the care of His disciple, John. Above all, He showed His love and mercy toward humanity by asking God to forgive those involved with the sin of His crucifixion.

Mercy should likewise be at the heart of mankind. The words of Jesus as given in the Beatitudes give cre-dence to this principle: "Blessed are the merciful: for they shall obtain mercy" (Matthew 5:7).

Mercy toward our fellow man opens the door for the blessings of God. Stay blessed.

D'Vinny

Day 48 | Repentance

"Have I any pleasure at all that the wicked should die? saith the Lord GOD: and not that he should return from his ways, and live?"

Ezekiel 18:23

The road to heaven begins with our repentance of sin.

D'Vinny

There is an innate human desire to live our own lives in our own way according to our own standards. Often times these standards are selfish because they center around the elevation of the individual over everything else. Many of these personal philosophies lead directly to sin:

"Look out for number one."
"Get while the getting is good."
"I have the money, so I make the rules."
"You only live once."
"All's fair in love and war."

Each of these axioms leads a person into direct conflict with God. Any time a person's desire is different than God's, the result is sin.

God sends messages from heaven to let us know when our behavior is off. The messages arrive in the kind, corrective voice of a family member or friend—or even a stranger. "Be not forgetful to entertain strangers; for thereby some have entertained angels unawares" (Hebrews 13:2). Messages can also come in dreams or events. A person could be traveling by car to a place he shouldn't be going. While *en route*, he could witness a tragic traffic accident right in front of him. This is the Holy Spirit of God letting the person know that he is on the road which leads to destruction, death, and hell.

The first thing that needs to happen is the person must realize that he is doing wrong in the sight of God. It is God who sets the standards for man's behavior, and only He has the divine authority to determine what is right and what is wrong. God wants all people to come to a state of repentance and live (see 1 Peter 3).

Each of us must realize that God expects and demands repentance. If we believe that we don't need to repent of anything, it is the same as saying we have not sinned. Thus, there is a void in our spiritual understanding. "He that covereth his sins shall not prosper but whoso confesseth and forsaketh them shall have mercy" (Proverbs 28:13).

It is only when we confess our sins unto God that He will be just and forgive us and will cleanse us spiritually from all unrighteousness.

Repentance is good medicine. Stay blessed.

D'Vinny

Day 49 | Work

"And whatsoever ye do, do it heartily, as to the Lord, and not unto men; Knowing that of the Lord ye shall receive the reward of the inheritance: for ye serve the Lord Christ."

Colossians 3:23-24

A non-working man is on the road to self-destruction.

D'Vinny

Work gives purpose and meaning to life: to use our talents, abilities, creative ideas, and collective positive energy for the benefit of society, family, and ourselves. Work in its various forms of occupation, academia, research, and entrepreneurialism allows individuals to be productive citizens and to add value to the world.

Our occupation helps to define us, especially when it is performed in a manner which is pleasing unto God. It is what we do for an honest living—and how well we do it—which brings honor to God. Moreover, in some respects a job will help shape our character. For example, an elementary school teacher must develop the attributes of patience, understanding, kindness, and nurturing; whereas a research biologist will require a slightly different skill set as he pursues the latest scientific breakthroughs.

Very often society will define individuals by their livelihood. Consider the question "who is she?" An answer is typically given by describing the person's profession—e.g., she is a doctor, accountant, counselor, or preacher. Her occupation is often given before her name.

God created us to work. The first man, Adam, was given the task of naming all the animals and serving as caretaker of the Garden of Eden (see Genesis 2). Therefore, man's first job was that of a gardener and environmentalist. Work became more difficult and required significant toil, when man sinned against God and was cast out of Eden, and the level of labor intensified (see Genesis 3).

Work which results from an honest living of sound morals is honorable and blessed by God. There is no such thing as a "Christian drug dealer" or an "honest bank robber." "Envy thou not the oppressor and choose none of his ways" (Proverbs 3:31). Everyone is required to perform well and work as though they are working for God and not for man.

It is God that we serve on the job, because He is the ultimate One who rewards the inheritance of all good things (see Colossians 3). Remember that every promotion at work comes from Him. God is the continuous supervisor who is always on duty.

May God bless the work we do and the lives we touch. Stay blessed.

D'Vinny

Day 50 | Scripture

"In the beginning was the Word, and the Word was with God, and the Word was God. The same was in the beginning with God."

John 1:1-2

Our scriptural life is the time in which God is speaking to us through His Word.

D'Vinny

The term *scripture* is used to refer to both the Holy Bible in its entirety as well as its individual books, chapters, and verses. It is God speaking to all of humanity, revealing Himself to us. Everything that man needs to know is given in the scripture. The Holy Bible gives instructions on marriage, family, personal behavior, social and legal justice, business conduct, finance, sickness, forgiveness, worship—the scripture is thoroughly comprehensive to meet all of our needs.

No other perfect book exists; only the Bible serves this purpose to the fullest extent. Both reading the scriptures and praying are important components of a person's religious life. Both must be done in harmony and on a continuous basis, and both are methods which enable us to communicate with God.

Prayer is a moment of serenity, a heartfelt conversation with God; and He expects us to pray, just as Jesus taught His disciples (see Matthew 6). While prayer is important, reading the scripture is equally so. The scripture reveals the true nature, character, and expectations of God, and all prayer is subsequently based upon the scripture, as well as the way we worship.

The most important events of our earthly existence, everything from birth to death, are all discussed in the scripture. Our time spent reading the Word of God should be the most precious time of our life.

Follow the scripture and remain within the territory of the Gospel. Stay blessed.

D'Vinny

"Come now, and let us reason together, saith the LORD: though your sins be as scarlet, they shall be as white as snow; though they be red like crimson, they shall be as wool. If ye be willing and obedient, ye shall eat the good of the land:"
Isaiah 1:18-19

Sin results when man does not follow the Word of God.
D'Vinny

Sin happens in one of two ways: *commission* or *omission*. The act of commission is simply to commit an act which is contrary to God's desire for human behavior. The act of lying is a sin, because God always expects the truth to be told (see Proverbs 6). The act of murder is a sin, as God stated in the Ten Commandments.

The act of omission is simply that of doing nothing in a situation when action is required. This is the case in the parable Jesus told of the Good Samaritan (see Luke 10). The first and second person, a priest and a Levite respectfully, both passed by an injured man, and both intentionally distanced themselves from him. The priest even moved to the other side of the road. These two able-bodied men committed a sin of omission by neglecting to provide first aid, care, or support. They decided not to inconvenience themselves and violated God's law of loving thy neighbor as thyself (see Romans 13).

The sin of omission also occurs when a person with malicious intent does not complete a task which God gives to them. The Bible records the Sin of Onan as an example (see Genesis 38), and the Sin of King Saul, concerning the Amalekite spoil, as another (see 1 Samuel 15).

God takes no pleasure when man uses his free will to act contrary to the Word of God. There is extreme spiritual conflict when a creature thinks his way is better than the way of his Creator. Essentially, all sin consists of selfish desire. There is an element of a self-centered individuality which is at its core. The Bible teaches that the final result of sin is death, and that the way to overcome it is through the Son of God (see Romans 6 and 1 Corinthians 15).

The alleviation of sin requires two components: *repentance* and *salvation*. Repentance means to renounce and turn away from sin with the intent to never repeat it. Salvation requires each individual to accept God's gift of saving his soul by coming into a personal relationship with Jesus Christ (see Acts 16). God's desire is for all sinning to cease and for the acts of wickedness to be replaced with righteousness (see Ezekiel 18)—to choose love over sin.

Sin and blessings from God cannot coexist; we must choose one or the other. Stay blessed.

D'Vinny

Day 52 | Prayer

"Pray without ceasing."

1 Thessalonians 5:17

When in doubt, remember that prayer is the most important thing we can do both today and tomorrow.

D'Vinny

We engage in many conversations on a daily basis. We talk with family members, friends, and co-workers in order to exchange ideas and receive necessary information. Communication is an essential aspect of survival in this world—both for humans and animals alike. Inherently, it is paramount that we communicate with God. This is vitally important for our physical and spiritual well-being. If an individual's soul does not stand right with God, he will not have inner peace. Therefore, communication with God through prayer must take place on a daily basis.

God expects prayer. God wants us to know that He is a loving Father who always has time to listen to our needs. God never gives us a busy signal, and He never gossips. Our sincere prayers are heard. We have God's confidentiality, His perfect privacy, when we bring our petitions, worries, and cares to Him. It is recorded that "the effectual fervent prayer of a righteous man availeth much" (James 5:16b).

Jesus, the Son of God, prayed. Jesus' longest prayer is when He prayed to God asking for glorification of the Father and for the spiritual well-being of His disciples (see John 17). He taught His disciples how to pray. He gave them a liturgical prayer, also known as the model prayer, which is commonly referred to as The Lord's

Prayer (see Matthew 6). Jesus prayed when He fed the multitude of 5,000 men and their wives and children (see Mark 6). When Jesus looked up to heaven and asked God's blessings upon the food, the standard was set for Christians to say a prayer of thanks before they eat a meal.

Jesus further gave an example of humility and forgiveness through prayer as He was dying on the cross. Jesus prayed, "Father forgive them; for they know not what they do" (Luke 23:34). Let us remember to have a life which includes daily conversations with God.

God answers our prayers. Stay blessed.

D'Vinny

Day 53 | Divorce

". . . Because the LORD hath been witness between thee and the wife of thy youth, against whom thou hast dealt treacherously: yet is she thy companion, and the wife of thy covenant. And did not he make one? . . . Therefore, take heed to your spirit, and let none deal treacherously against the wife of his youth."

Malachi 2:14-15

The more "self" there is in a marriage, the less room is left for God.

D'Vinny

The view of man is that marriage can be ended with divorce so that a person can move on with his life. It has become ubiquitous throughout the modern world. Nevertheless, this is man's social practice; it is not the Will of God.

God did not create marriage for it to become easily dissolved by divorce. Marriage is the expectation of God, His holy plan, whereby one male and one female will make a solemn and righteous vow to each other. Before God, they swear that they will love, honor, protect, and obey until death.

Whenever difficulties and problems should occur, God did not intend a back door to be left open just in case one person would like to give up. Instead of paying legal fees and court costs, we must turn to committed prayer, fasting, and spiritual rededication unto God, through His Son, Jesus. This is how the flame of original love in the marriage is to be rekindled, putting the concept of divorce out of each person's spirit.

Divorce is caused by sin, by a desire to do things our own way instead of God's way. We explain that financial suffering pushed us toward divorce. God says that money cannot break up a marriage if the vows of "for richer or poorer" are taken seriously. We say that if the Joneses have it, we have to have it. God says: "But seek ye first the kingdom of God, and his righteousness; and all these things shall be added unto you" (Matthew 6:33). Society says revenge is sweet and there is nothing like payback. God says: "Be not overcome by evil but overcome evil with good" (Romans 12:21).

The spiritual understanding, we are to reach is that every aspect of divorce only serves to distance man from God. Alternate lifestyles, pre-nuptial agreements, unfaithfulness, excessive materialism, relentless pride, and other forms of sin lead us down a dark path. The divorce problem can only be solved when man attempts to adopt a Godly mindset and to not allow the conditions of divorce to exist in the first place.

Only God can keep a marriage together, because God created marriage. Stay blessed.

D'Vinny

Day 54 | Offerings

"And all the tithe of the land, whether of the seed of the land, or of the fruit of the tree, is the LORD's: it is holy unto the LORD."

Leviticus 27:30

An offering is a spiritual use of God's money.

D'Vinny

Everything that we have in both the spiritual and physical world is a blessing from God. Money comes from God, and He expects us to use it in a wise manner. One of the wisest ways to do this is to employ it as an instrument of worship.

Each person must realize that in an offering we are giving God back a part of what already belongs to Him. It is the religious praise of God's money, conditioning us to show love, respect, and humility toward Him. It is an act of obedience and self-control, and it allows man to come closer to his Creator. Most churches and places of worship will take a collection. This allows the congregation to spiritually focus on God and to thank Him for His blessings and grace.

Yet, God does not accept all offerings. Cain's offering was rejected by God (see Genesis 4), as was King Saul's (see 1 Samuel 15). An offering requires obedience and the right spirit. God does not want those that have been given with a reluctant attitude, arrogance, or stinginess. Sadly, it is in this part of the Christian experience that so many come up short. They want to keep 100% of their money as opposed to having 90% along with the blessings of God. Therefore, they will cheat God and only give him the leftovers of their financial successes, instead of bringing God a proportionate share. One cannot serve two masters—God and money. It is one or the other.

An offering as an act of worship allows a Christian character to be developed. It elevates our relationship with God while simultaneously reducing our dependence on material objects. Holy living is a requirement of God (see Leviticus 19). Nothing should lessen a humble servant's desire to render the right attitude and offerings unto God, so He may accept them according to His word in the Holy Bible.

God blesses our offerings when we present them humbly. Stay blessed.

D'Vinny

Day 55 | Pride

"The pride of thine heart hath deceived thee, thou that dwellest in the clefts of the rock, whose habitation is high; that saith in his heart, who shall bring me down to the ground?"

Obadiah 1:3

Pride is the beginning of all sin.

D'Vinny

Pride is used by Satan to artificially inflate man's motives, desires, and obsession with self-actualization. It is a state of mind that separates us from God's will, often referred to as the root cause of other forms of sin. Pride is a form of arrogance which tells the ego that it cannot be limited, cannot be denied, and that self-satisfaction must be achieved at all costs—resulting in a "god complex." A prideful person wishes to control each and every situation.

For example, when both persons in a marriage are full of pride, conflict is often rampant. The smallest issues are blown out of proportion, each person attempting to impose his or her will over the other. Likewise, nations will not follow logical reasoning and sound judgment because of prideful arrogance, often entering warfare when it is unnecessary and orienting themselves in a direction away from God. Throughout history, great kingdoms have fallen because of national pride and the need for a people to demonstrate hegemony over their neighbors.

The sin of pride gives way to a state of denial, a refusal to admit one has done wrong. This is what happens when superpowers attempt to homogenize the world around them, to impose their own systems of government and economics upon other nations. The path away from pride is for all nations to live peaceably with each other by following the will, desires, and expectations of God. If all were to submit themselves unto God, then pride would be eliminated at the international level and peace would be given a chance to prevail.

God will not let any one nation gain too much control for very long. It is God who lifts them up—and it is God who brings them down.

The arrogance of pride is demonic in nature; it gets in the way of God's blessings. Stay blessed.

D'Vinny

Day 56 | Music

"And it came to pass, when the evil spirit from God was upon Saul, that David took an harp, and played with his hand: so Saul was refreshed, and was well, and the evil spirit departed from him."

1 Samuel 16:23

Music must be kept clean, for it belongs to God.

D'Vinny

Music is a beautiful form of art that was created by God, an expression of the soul which demonstrates His glory. It can communicate for the individual what the mere utterance of words cannot. There are a wide variety of styles which can be found in every culture; there is neither a tribe nor a nation without its own form of music.

It is universal, because music has a direct appeal to the senses. The sound of an organ or piano when played by a skilled craftsman, will ease listeners into a state of comfort—as will the vibrations from a bass drum, the twang of a guitar, and the mellifluous sound of a saxophone. Yet, mankind has handed certain forms of music over to Satan. When the devil gets into music, he alters the intended purpose of God. The devil was formerly the chief of the angelic host when he was in heaven. Therefore, he uses music as a tool to manipulate us toward sin. The phrase "sex, drugs, and rock-n-roll" was designed by Lucifer, the great deceiver of mankind.

The expression of music must be without sin. It must always remain above reproach, so that the Lord can bless the music as a lasting work of art—as well as bless the musician. The sight of a marching band playing "When the Saints Go Marching In" foreshadows our entrance into heaven, by a long line of people who died in Christ with their sins forgiven. Music is special when it is used to give praise unto God. Religious music exists within many genres—country, classical, gospel, rock, etc.—and no one style has importance over any other. All sincere, heartfelt music is pleasing to God, especially when it is used spiritually.

It is important for Christians to keep music positive and acceptable unto God. There are problems with certain types of music that contain unholy lyrics, profanity, or insults. This is improper use of one of His gifts.

Use music to praise God and He will bless accordingly. Stay blessed.

D'Vinny

Day 57 | Environment

"He stood, and measured the earth: he beheld, and drove asunder the nations; and the everlasting mountains were scattered, the perpetual hills did bow: his ways are everlasting."

Habakkuk 3:6

The environment represents the divine craftsmanship of God.

D'Vinny

The environment is a synonym for the planet on which we live. God designed heaven and earth upon holy wisdom and announced that everything that He had made was very good (see Genesis 1). The world has been tailored by God for man, made to contain everything we need for physical life. God intended for the environment to endure into perpetuity.

However, this world was changed by original sin. Paradise was compromised, and man and his environment became adversaries—thus we have earthquakes, hurricanes, floods, and other perils of nature. The present-day concern is the destruction of the environment through pollution and carbon emissions. As society becomes more industrialized and technologically advanced, the regulation of toxic emissions into the environment needs to be addressed. An undesirable halo of smog hangs upon the crown of many of the world's most developed cities, our rivers are dirty, and our soil is contaminated.

God expects for mankind to take care and show respect, appreciation, and gratefulness for the wonderful home which He has given us. The scripture is still true:

no man can serve two masters (Matthew 6:24). Often times, profit and environmental conservation are at odds with each other, but a respectable level of economic prosperity can be achieved without the destruction of our most precious capital asset: earth. This home is one that man cannot replace, for it was provided by a kind and caring God.

Collectively, it is up to us to set environmental standards to ensure that pollution is minimized to the lowest possible level. The environment is not to be taken lightly. Care for the environment is one of man's ways to render proper thanks, praise, and appreciation to our Creator.

Respect shown to our natural surroundings is respect shown unto God. Stay blessed.

D'Vinny

Day 58 | Suicide

"And when Ahithophel saw that his counsel was not followed, he saddled his ass, and arose, and gat him home to his house, to his city, and put his household in order, and hanged himself, and died, and was buried in the sepulchre of his father."

2 Samuel 17:23

Suicide is a permanent mistake that solves nothing.

D'Vinny

We do not choose when we are going to be born. That decision was made by God. Likewise, we do not get to choose when we should die. The issues of life and death belong solely to God, and it is only He who has the power and responsibility to pronounce the end of a person's journey.

The reasons why people commit suicide are many. It has been said that it is a "permanent solution to a temporary problem." We must remember that time has a special way of ameliorating the factors that cause thoughts of suicide. We must also remember that it is a violation of the Ten Commandments: "Thou shalt not kill" (Exodus 20). This scripture is applicable, not only to the killing of one's neighbor, but also to the killing of oneself. When a person commits suicide, he is actually playing god. We must have the faith to understand that no problem is too hard for Him (see Genesis 18). We may have big problems, but we need to remember that we have a bigger God to whom we can go for healing, understanding, and renewed strength.

Suicide is an emotional issue, especially for those who have lost family members or friends. It permanently halts the process of reconciliation and forgiveness due to the chasm caused by death. God did not intend for any problem to create so much stress that one of His children would feel that life was worthless. He wants us to face each difficulty with courage, conviction, and strength as exemplified by His Son, Jesus. God does not want us to give up.

There is a school of thought that suicide is an unforgivable sin. The rationale is that after the sin is committed a person cannot ask God for forgiveness. The Bible does not teach this philosophy. This train of thought comes from the reasoning of man. The important thing is to provide assistance to those who are in need. Medical aid to help treat depression and post-traumatic stress will help. Likewise, it is important for the neighbors of the Christian to be observant, to recognize signs of suicidal intention. "Bear ye one another's burdens, and so fulfill the law of Christ" (Galatians 6:2).

The family, the church, and a solid support system can bring a person to Jesus Christ, the Son of God. There is no problem that Jesus cannot solve.

Give life a chance and see the resulting blessings from God. Stay blessed.

D'Vinny

Day 59 | Preaching

"And I will give you pastors according to mine heart, which shall feed you with knowledge and understanding."

Jeremiah 3:15

Righteous preaching comes from God.

D'Vinny

It is God who calls men and women into the ministry. All preachers are responsible to God, and He will hold them accountable for the content of their sermons. The objective of preaching is to get a sinful man to stop sinning, repent of his evil ways, turn to God, and receive God's free gift of salvation through His Son Jesus—thus securing a place for his soul in heaven.

It is the Holy Bible that has the power to convert, redeem, and restore, but the ability to preach the Word with conviction comes from God. Therefore, all preachers must remain in prayer before and during sermon preparation. This special prayer time is to ensure that the preacher's spirit touches God's Spirit, so that a holy anointing can take place before the sermon is given.

Heaven is pleased when sermons are sound and evangelical in nature. All homilies must be effective in that the audience is able to hear, remember, and understand what was said. This is known as homiletics—the art of preaching. Although styles vary, it is important to connect the audience to the preacher who is in turn connected to God. The second aspect is evangelism, which is drawing people to Jesus. It is Jesus, the Son of God, who is our High Priest in heaven (see Hebrews 4). Jesus is the One who allows a sinful man to be made right with God, and all sermons must draw people to Christ.

There exists a problem in preaching today, known as "prosperity preaching." This teaches that the person who gives will be rewarded by God with more money. Certainly, there is an element of truth to this statement; however, the act of financial giving has been taken out of context. It is understandable that the church needs funding in order to cover their basic costs, such as: utilities, insurance, training materials, maintenance, etc. However, the question has to be asked, "How much money is enough?" The danger of prosperity preaching is that the preacher and the congregation slowly begin to drift away from the † symbol and drift toward the $ symbol.

Preaching only exists on earth. There will be no preaching in heaven; because, in heaven there will be no need to tell people to stop sinning and come to God. Man will already be with God. The Word will be made complete and internalized in the souls of those in heaven.

Grow spiritually with good preaching and sound religious doctrine. Stay blessed.

D'Vinny

Day 60 | Government

"Then Solomon sat on the throne of the LORD as king instead of David his father, and prospered; and all Israel obeyed him."

1 Chronicles 29:23

Government works best when God leads the administration.

D'Vinny

God values structure and organization in society, from the family echelon on up to the national and international levels, and he subsequently established government. The Bible teaches: "Let all things be done decently and in order" (1 Corinthians 14:40). Society cannot exist without order. Government prevents chaos and anarchy through the design and enforcement of laws, regulations, and standards. The advancement of society—through education, sanitation, housing, health care, security, etc.—depends upon strong leadership and organization.

It is clear there are many challenges that governments face, especially in third world nations. Many of these governments have problems with corruption, political instability, and difficulty providing basic needs and services to their citizens. An example would be the country of Somalia. This country has struggled for decades to establish postal and banking systems, with little success. Internal problems with warlords vying for power, violence, and economic stagnancy have kept Somalis in relative destitution.

Indeed, there is much work that needs to be done around the world to help nations eliminate poverty and to provide a sound social structure. Reduction of both internal and external conflict is needed to move forward as a global community.

We are required to pray for the governmental leaders. This biblical mandate is given in 1 Timothy 2:2 to pray for "kings, and for all that are in authority; that we may lead a quiet and peaceable life in all godliness and honesty." The people in government need our spiritual support to fight the pressures to pursue selfish financial gain by the oppression of the citizenry.

It is God who elevates nations and governments; likewise, it is the same God who reduces the power and influence of these countries, especially when they become too haughty, corrupt, or sinful. All are to serve and honor God, to please him with their policies and laws.

There will be a final government. It will come from God through His Son, Jesus. Isaiah recorded: ". . . the government shall be upon his shoulder; and his name shall be called Wonderful, Counsellor, The mighty God, The everlasting Father, The Prince of Peace. Of the increase of his government and peace there shall be no end . . ." (Isaiah 9:6-7). The various national governments of man are temporary, and we have the assurance that something better is coming. "And I saw a new heaven and a new earth: for the first heaven and the first earth were passed away . . ." (Revelation 21:1).

Ask God for the blessing of a righteous government. Stay blessed.

D'Vinny

Day 61 | Trials

"But and if ye suffer for righteousness' sake, happy are ye: and be not afraid of their terror, neither be troubled."

1 Peter 3:14

Every trial is an opportunity to build character and strengthen our faith in God.

D'Vinny

Something that disappoints God is the lack of religious perseverance some people exhibit when they are faced with a difficult situation. People of faith tend to practice their religious beliefs when things are going well in their lives. However, when negative experiences happen, their faith and trust in Him sometimes wavers. God wants consistency, not just to be worshipped and served when times are good.

Moses' life was filled with trials. At birth, he was placed in a basket and set adrift on the Nile. He appeared before the Pharaoh during the time of the Ten Plagues with a message from God to "let my people go." Likewise, Moses' military victory at the Red Sea, as led by the Hand of God, was a difficult experience. One of the greatest armies in history had to be destroyed.

In turn, each of the prophets went through multiple trials when God called them to deliver His Word to the world. Isaiah walked naked for three years (see Isaiah 20) as a sign of pending disaster, because of the sin involving idolatry of the nation. Jeremiah was beaten and placed in iron shackles (see Jeremiah 20) for preaching and prophesying God's message. Later, he was imprisoned in a muddy well, known as a cistern, and had to be rescued from certain death. Daniel was set before the lions because of his devoted act of daily prayer (see Daniel 6). Hosea was instructed by God to marry a prostitute named Gomer (see Hosea 1). This was to symbolize that Israel had become an unfaithful and untrusting nation in its relationship with God. Nonetheless, God would later institute a plan to reconcile His people back to Him in a harmonious relationship of grace and love.

God does not expect us to lose faith nor to run from our problems. God's desire is not to abandon us when we most need Him, but rather to bring us through it all so that we may give testimony to His saving grace. The key to remember is that there is a blessing for us to receive from God whenever we are in a rough spot. The bad times will not last. These are periods of refinement and spiritual conditioning. God expects for these experiences to make us stronger by drawing us closer to Him.

Trials have been a part of life ever since mankind lost the paradise of Eden. Therefore, when natural disasters occur, all people of faith must remember to stay with God. When a job loss or bankruptcy should occur, God wants us to know that it is not the end of the world. When a medical condition should take a turn for the worse, and good health is not to be found, we must realize that God is still in control, because God is the One who made the body.

Our faith must be strong enough to assure us that, regardless of the circumstances, God is too righteous, too wise, and too powerful to make a mistake. Time itself brings trials along with it, as we experience them when we age. Our requirement, as stated by Jesus is:

"Be thou faithful unto death and I will give thee a crown of life" (Revelation 2:10).

God's blessings are greater than any trial or tribulation. Stay blessed.

D'Vinny

Day 62 | Failure

"I opened to my beloved; but my beloved had with-drawn himself, and was gone: my soul failed when he spake: I sought him, but I could not find him; I called him, but he gave me no answer."

Song of Solomon 5:6

Not getting to heaven is the only true failure.

D'Vinny

We like success. Accepting a gold medal in the Olympics Games is typically a great joy. A business deal that has been successfully closed or the ground-breaking ceremony for a new multimillion-dollar facili-ty are examples of accomplished goals or victories.

Needless to say, even given our best attempt and a steadfast work ethic, sometimes we will fall short of the mark. No one has the Midas Touch, where every en-deavor he undertakes is a shining success. Failure hap-pens. It is important to differentiate between experienc-ing failure and internalizing failure. When we experi-ence failure, it is external; conversely, when we become a failure, it is internal. The latter causes depression and feelings of worthlessness. Thus, it is important to re-member that one can fail without *being* a failure.

They let us know that we need God. Maybe in the next iteration of the undertaking, we need to include spiritual preparation as well as the physical, financial, and academic preparation. One famous surgeon would always stop by the hospital chapel to have a quiet talk with God in prayer before he went into the operation room for surgery. The doctor knew that even though many hours were spent in research and preparation for the long, complex neurosurgical operation, God needed some of his time. Moreover, the doctor understood that every patient in his career would not survive every operation—that death was a possibility. But he knew there was no failure in God.

Failure is a tool, which if kept in proper perspective, can humble our spirit and recalibrate our soul. It allows our pride to remain in check, and to help keep us connected with God. Failure is not a reason to capitulate. God expects us to continue trying, not to quit. When we work, we must realize that we work for God (see Colossians 2).

Additionally, there is a difference between man's view of failure and God's. Society often associates failure with not achieving wealth, fame, or power, but God always looks at the condition of the soul. "For my thoughts are not your thoughts, neither are your ways my ways, saith the Lord" (Isaiah 55:8). Failure to complete a task is not the end; it is another opportunity. Sometimes God uses these missteps to get our attention and to direct us toward another path in life. Viewed in a similar manner, death is not failure; it is a tool used by God to invite a faithful soul into heaven to enjoy eternal oneness with the Creator. There is no failure in God's fellowship.

God blesses us despite our shortcomings. Stay blessed.

D'Vinny

Day 63 | Sex

"And she said unto him, How canst thou say, I love thee, when thine heart is not with me? . . . And it came to pass, when she pressed him daily with her words, and urged him, so that his soul was vexed unto death."

Judges 16:15

Only God has the perfect plan for humanity.

D'Vinny

God created sex for procreation of the human species. God's will is for sex to be a compassionate expression of love between a man and a woman who are joined by holy matrimony, allowing for the creation of the most fundamental aspect of society: the family.

Man is still trying to uncover the mysteries of sex through research and analysis, but God knows everything there is to know about the subject. Even though enormous volumes have been written, and an endless number of surveys have been conducted, man largely remains in a state of perplexed bewilderment concerning the matter. Man is confused because he doesn't acknowledge that sex belongs to God. It is a gift. Although sex is physical, it must be understood on a spiritual level—in other words, the former must be subordinate to the latter. This will allow all sexual activity to be placed where it belongs, which is under the guidance of the Holy Spirit.

Many examples of the disastrous effects of sexual deviation can be found in the Bible. Lot's daughters decided to get their father drunk and impregnate themselves, thus having children from incest (see Genesis 19). Sarai (later changed to Sarah), the wife of Abra-

137

ham, due to her impatience and lack of faith in God's plan, gave her personal servant Hagar to her husband Abraham to have continuous sex with until Hagar became pregnant (see Genesis 16). This act catalyzed the series of events that created the tension between Jews and Arabs, both of whom are descended from the same father.

Samson, the world's strongest man, let sex with a woman named Delilah—whose name means "to desire"—cause him to break his covenant with God (see Judges 16). Likewise, the world's richest man, King Solomon, let seven hundred wives and princesses and three hundred concubines cause him to turn away from God (see 1 Kings 11). King Solomon collected women as a hobby. Spiritually, this was his undoing.

Our present-day society has encountered a barrage of sexual problems: child molestation, rape, sexually transmitted diseases, adultery, teen pregnancies, abortion, unwed mothers, homosexuality, pornography, etc. These, as well as all other devious sexual acts, are a result of man's self-direction, personal influence, and individualism toward the subject. The sexual revolution has hurt more than it has helped, introducing recreational sex as "the norm." The flawed logic of sexual liberty forgets that sexual desire, when left unchecked, can never be fully satiated. It is always off to seek the next thrill, while often times leading people to their graves.

Anything in life—an idea, belief, or practice—that is outside the will of God is sinful. Although society continues to try, it cannot solve these problems. Only God can, once humanity is willing to humble itself and entirely hand the concept of sex over to Him.

Sex is a blessing only when God is in control. Stay blessed.

D'Vinny

Day 64 | Drugs

"Beloved, follow not that which is evil, but that which is good. He that doeth good is of God: but he that doeth evil hath not seen God."

3 John 1:11

An appetite for drugs is an appetite for death.

D'Vinny

There is no question that illegal drugs have a negative impact upon society. As drug usage has increased over the years, so has crime. Many people who commit armed robbery, burglary, shoplifting, and identify theft are doing so to feed an addiction.

Drug addicts are caught within a catch-22. They know the difference between right and wrong; however, drugs have a way of rewiring minds, elevating the importance of feeding the addiction over all else. This is why, if given the choice, an addict will use his last twenty dollars to buy drugs instead of food, shelter, or some other necessity. The Apostle Paul, author of most of the New Testament, understood this paradox from a spiritual perspective. He recorded in Romans 7:19: "For the good that I would, I do not: but the evil which I would not, that I do."

Theologically speaking, use of illegal drugs is not of God, but rather a tool of Satan. The devil is able to use every aspect of the drug trade for his nefarious work. This is clearly seen in the broken lives of street pushers and users, after Satan uses drugs to seize control over their minds, to induce destructive behavior.

Individuals enter the drug trade because of the quick, tax-free cash to be made—but no one should be this easily deceived. The Word of God clearly teaches: "Envy thou not the oppressor; and choose none of his ways" (Proverbs 3:31). There is no such thing as a Christian drug dealer. God understands difficult economic circumstances, but the loss of a job is no justification to pursue any kind of occupation or lifestyle that is deliberately harmful to others.

Society has an irrational desire to get stoned. Typically, a user is introduced to drugs by his friends. There is a desire to fit in or to belong with the crowd—or simply just to feel different. Parents must know who their children's friends are; and they must have an idea of their character. "Be not deceived: evil communications corrupt good manners" (1 Corinthians 15:33). Additionally, parents must keep their own behavior and personal conduct above reproach by being drug free, because they set the first example for their children.

We cannot, solely of our own power, withstand every wicked temptation of Satan. Satan knows each desire and weakness of man. But, there is hope. Our refuge is God. "Submit yourselves therefore to God. Resist the devil, and he will flee from you" (James 4:7), and remember that, "For ye are bought with a price: therefore, glorify God in your body and in your spirit which we are God's" (1 Corinthians 6:20).

Avoid drugs, because they are one of the tools of Satan. Stay blessed.

D'Vinny

Day 65 | Tragedy

"Is any among you afflicted? let him pray."

James 5:13a

Let tragedy allow us to move closer to God.

D'Vinny

Life has its ups and downs, its stressful moments followed by stretches of tranquility. Things tend to follow a consistent pattern of work, school, family time, chores, and religious activity. But sometimes our normal routine will become disrupted by tragic events beyond our control.

A tragedy can strike at any time, as when it did on September 11, 2001. Four commercial passenger aircraft were hijacked by terrorists. The pilots were killed and the terrorists steered the vehicles to a fiery, destructive end. Two of the aircraft hit the Twin Towers of the World Trade Center in New York City. The terrorist used the airplanes as deadly aerial missiles which resulted in a massive explosion, instantly killing all the passengers on board as well as many office workers inside the buildings as well as on the ground. The first shock was the initial impact; the second shock was the actual collapse of each tower.

In Washington, D.C., another symbol of a strong and prosperous nation was attacked—the world's largest office building, the Pentagon. Due to the structure and limited height of the Pentagon, the damage was contained to one side of the building. Total destruction did not occur, but there was nevertheless loss of life and personal injury, in addition to the property destruction.

The final hijacked aircraft did not reach its intended target. A few brave passengers overtook the airplane from the terrorists, and the plane crashed in a wooded Pennsylvania forest. No one survived, but the courageous heroism of the passengers prevented the continuation of even more cataclysmic terror.

After these events, there was a chiasmic spiritual void in the hearts of many people. Some people questioned why God did not intercede. The facial expressions of the lost and bewildered seemed to cry out, "Where is God?" Amidst the confusion and dismay, God is always right there. "The earth is the Lord's, and the fullness thereof; the world, and they that dwell therein" (Psalms 24:1). God has not given the world totally over to evil. God has all things under His control. We have been instructed through the words of Proverbs 16:14: "The Lord hath made all things for himself: yea, even the wicked for the day of evil." We must remember that God is still in charge.

Many tragedies that occur are caused by man—arson, suicide bombings, assassinations, mass shootings, drunk drivers, genocide, etc. These are the results of the Word of God not being followed. The requirement from God has not changed: ". . . Thou shalt love thy neighbor as thyself" (Galatians 5:14). Also in the same chapter we find: "Let us not be desirous of vain glory, provoking one, another envying one another" (Galatians 5:26).

Man-made tragedy occurs when humanitarianism and the Scriptures are forgotten. "For we wrestle not against flesh and blood, but against principalities and, powers, against the rulers of the darkness of this world, against spiritual wickedness in high places" (Ephesians 6:12). Yes, the shocking events of 9/11 were indeed a terrible tragedy caused by the forces of evil. God intervened to prevent even more aircraft from being hi-jacked, and He did not allow the fourth airplane to hit its target.

We must have the faith, knowledge, and conviction that God can overcome anything. Every tragedy gives us the opportunity, even during the most unnerving of times, to be still and to allow the quiet Voice of God to minister to our spirits. The words of the childhood religious song are still true: "He's Got the Whole World in His Hands".

No tragedy can stop God's love. Stay blessed.
D'Vinny

Day 66 | Revelation

"I am Alpha and Omega, the beginning and the ending, saith the Lord, which is, and which was, and which is to come, the Almighty."

Revelation 1:8

Why live like there is no tomorrow when Jesus is returning tomorrow?

D'Vinny

There is one known truth about our life on earth: it is very short. The Bible gives the comparison that our lives are as brief as the appearance, duration, and scope of water vapor (see James 4). Why are we so concerned about our life on earth when it composes only a sliver of our entire existence? There is a significant connection between our earthly life and our spiritual life afterwards. It is in the things that we do, the way that we live, and in our true relationship with God—or an absence thereof—that will determine whether the soul will be in heaven with God, the heavenly host, or will spend eternity in the confines of hell with the other lost souls.

Each day on earth must be lived as if, the very next day, we will find ourselves standing before God. Everyone is going to heaven—but not everyone will stay. The soul will go before God to be held accountable for the things which were done while on earth. Likewise, there will come a time when the entire world will be held accountable unto God. This will happen at the "Second Epiphany"—the return of Christ.

Jesus' first epiphany was as a baby born in Bethlehem. He was the One who healed the sick, raised the dead, forgave sins, and taught humanity how to live. Jesus preached the Gospel and gave His life as a ransom for many (see Mark 10). He died, was buried, resurrected, and ascended into heaven where He sits at the right hand of the Father.

There are few things in life that are guaranteed. The second coming of Jesus is one of them. In the scripture we learn that Jesus will come back to earth, although He expressed that no one knows when (see Matthew 24). Our job is to be ready, to allow our faith to reassure us that the world is in His hands. The best way to prepare for the second coming is to follow the scriptures and have a proper relationship with God and with our fellow man (see Matthew 22). We must have an unconditional love for God which is binding in Jesus, and we must love our neighbor as we love ourselves.

The Second Epiphany will be much different from the first. Jesus will not be returning as a humble servant of man. He is coming back as King of Kings, and Lord of Lords. When Jesus returns the entire world will know it. The world will see the sky and the heaven open, the voices of archangels will be heard (1 Thessalonians 4).

Eschatology is the branch of theology which deals with the study of the last days and the final events which are to come. The most detailed account of scripture in regard to the last days are given in the Book of Revelation—which is appropriately the last book of the Bible. Its twenty-two chapters are filled with symbols and descriptive imagery of the things to come. The Revelation by Jesus Christ was given to the Apostle John while he was shipwrecked on the Island of Patmos off the coast of Asia Minor, which is known as the country of Turkey. The Bible is clear throughout, but Revelation makes it plain that this world is not our permanent home.

Satan is designated as the prince of this world, but he knows that his time is short. Satan will lose in his fight against God, known as the Battle of Armageddon and will thereafter have to face judgement from God (see Revelation 16). The apocalyptic events as described in the Bible should bring joy and not fear to the spirit of a Christian, for the work of the Lord must be done. Christians who have a relationship with Christ should always continue to take comfort in Him, at all times. He will undo the nefarious works which Satan has done unto mankind. Christ is our hope (see Romans 5).

The second coming of Christ will bring joy to the righteous. Therefore, all behavior, thoughts, and attitudes should be pleasing to the eyes of God in heaven so that we will remain in a state of blessedness. We are travelers heading to a better place. True health, true riches, true joy, true peace, and the true blessings of prosperity are not here. They are in heaven with our Loving and Everlasting Father.

Let nothing on earth come into conflict with the blessings of God.

I am humbly yours,

D'Vinny

THE END
AMEN

DAY	TITLE	SCRIPTURE
1	Marriage	Genesis 2:22
2	Love	I John 4:16
3	Salvation	Romans 10:9-10
4	Table Grace	St. Mark 6:41
5	Disappointment	I Corinthians 15:58
6	Friendship	II Kings 8:29b
7	Crime	Hosea 4:2
8	Benediction	Numbers 6: 24-26
9	Lying	II John 7
10	Money	I Timothy 6:10
11	Wisdom	II Peter 3:15
12	Joy	Nehemiah 8:10
13	Patience	Ecclesiastes 7:8
14	Parenting	Ruth 1:2
15	Death	Psalm of Death
16	Thy Neighbor	Galatians 5:14
17	Anxiety	Jonah 2:5
18	Greed	Jude 11
19	Stripping	Proverbs 29:3
20	Angels	II Thessalonians 1:7
21	Success	Joshua 1:8
22	Mentorship	Titus 2:12
23	Leadership	Exodus 32:34a
24	Alcohol	Ephesians 5:18
25	Cursing	II Timothy 2:16
26	Education	Ezra 7:10
27	Forgiveness	St. Matthew 6:14
28	Meekness	Zephaniah 2:3
29	Hope	Acts 24:15a
30	Worship	Joel 1:14
31	Negotiations	II Chronicles 7:14
32	Land Mines	Deuteronomy 5:17
33	Words	Zechariah 1:13

24	Superpower	Daniel 2:20-21
35	Decisions	I Kings 18:21
36	Inspiration	Job 32:8
37	Justice	Amos 5:24
38	Faith	Hebrews 11:1
39	War	Micah 4:3
40	Thankfulness	Philemon 4
41	God	Nahum 1:7
42	Poverty	II Corinthians 8:9
43	Homeless	St. Luke 9:58
44	Honesty	Philippians 4:8
45	Family	Esther 9:28
46	Materialism	Haggai 1:6
47	Mercy	Lamentations 3:22
48	Repent	Ezekiel 18:23
49	Work	Colossians 3:23-24
50	Scripture	St. John 1:1-2
51	Sin	Isaiah 1:18
52	Prayer	I Thessalonians 5:17
53	Divorce	Malachi 2:14-15
54	Offering	Leviticus 27:30
55	Pride	Obadiah 3
56	Music	I Samuel 16:23
57	Environment	Habakkuk 3:6
58	Suicide	II Samuel 17:23
59	Preaching	Jeremiah 3:15
60	Government	I Chronicles 29:23
61	Trails	I Peter 3:14
62	Failure	Song of Solomon 5:6
63	Sex	Judges 16:15
64	Drugs	III John 11
65	Tragedy	Romans 8:38-39
	Revelation	
66		Revelation 1:8

TABLE OF CONTENTS